Embedded Rust Essentials

Unlock Safe and Efficient Embedded Systems
Development for Real-World Applications

Jose Gobert

Copyright Page

Table of Contents

Preface

Embedded systems have always demanded precision, reliability, and efficiency. From the microcontrollers that regulate automotive systems and medical devices, to the tiny chips inside wearables and IoT sensors, these platforms power the physical world in silence. But developing for them has traditionally been associated with unsafe memory management, fragile toolchains, and error-prone C or assembly codebases. Too often, developers find themselves trading safety for performance, or struggling to enforce architectural discipline without language-level guarantees.

That trade-off ends with Rust.

Rust brings to embedded programming what's long been missing—**guaranteed memory safety without garbage collection**, **zero-cost abstractions**, **powerful concurrency**, and an expressive type system that turns entire classes of bugs into compile-time errors. In short, Rust enables you to write embedded code that is **safe, fast, and fearless**.

This book was written for developers who want to **build reliable, production-grade embedded systems using Rust**. Whether you're a seasoned embedded developer who's frustrated with the pitfalls of C, or a Rustacean curious about low-level systems work, this book is designed to meet you at your current level and guide you step by step through the essentials of embedded Rust programming.

You won't just blink LEDs—you'll learn to write reusable drivers, handle hardware interrupts safely, build real-time applications, and communicate with peripherals over UART, I2C, and SPI. You'll explore how Rust's `no_std` model works, how to configure microcontroller registers with peripheral access crates (PACs), and how to flash and debug code with modern tooling. You'll learn to manage power, log data from sensors, and package your applications for deployment—all using the safety guarantees and modern tooling that Rust provides.

Importantly, this book doesn't assume you're already an expert in embedded systems or Rust. Concepts are introduced gradually and explained clearly, without skipping the why behind the how. Real-world examples and complete working code are provided throughout, so you can not only follow along but also build on them in your own projects.

The structure of the book is designed to give you a foundation first, then help you build progressively more complex and capable systems:

You'll begin by understanding embedded systems and why Rust is uniquely suited to them.

You'll then set up your toolchain, pick your hardware, and build your first bare-metal firmware.

As you advance, you'll gain hands-on experience with peripherals, concurrency, power management, and project architecture.

In later chapters, you'll explore real-world applications, advanced tooling, and the future of embedded Rust.

This book also emphasizes practical development workflows. Debugging techniques, real-time considerations, testing strategies, and maintainable code structure are discussed in-depth to ensure you're not just writing code that works—you're writing code that lasts.

In the spirit of community, this book also reflects and draws from the excellent work being done across the Embedded Rust ecosystem. From `embedded-hal` to `RTIC`, from `probe-rs` to `defmt`, the tools and libraries discussed in these chapters are open-source, battle-tested, and improving every day thanks to a vibrant and growing community.

You are not alone on this path. Thousands of developers are turning to Rust to bring safety and structure to embedded systems development. With this book, you'll join them—not just by learning the language, but by **putting it to work in real-world embedded applications**.

Thank you for picking up *Embedded Rust Essentials*. I hope this book challenges, inspires, and empowers you to build systems that are not only powerful and performant—but provably safe.

Let's get to it.

Chapter 1: Embedded Systems and Rust

What Are Embedded Systems?

An embedded system is a specialized computing system that performs a dedicated function within a larger mechanical or electrical system. Unlike general-purpose computers, which are designed to handle a wide range of tasks and run multiple applications, an embedded system is purpose-built to carry out a specific task or set of closely related tasks. It often operates under tight constraints such as limited memory, processing power, storage capacity, or energy availability.

At the core of most embedded systems is a microcontroller—a compact integrated circuit that includes a processor (CPU), memory (RAM and flash), and peripherals like timers, GPIO (general-purpose input/output) pins, communication interfaces (such as UART, SPI, I2C), and analog-to-digital converters. These components work together to sense the environment, process inputs, and control outputs, enabling the device to interact with the physical environment.

Embedded systems are used in a wide variety of applications. In consumer electronics, they are found in devices like washing machines, smart thermostats, fitness trackers, and televisions. In industrial settings, they control robotic arms, monitor temperatures, and manage real-time safety systems. In automotive contexts, they are responsible for functions such as anti-lock braking, airbag deployment, and infotainment systems. Medical devices, avionics, and infrastructure equipment all rely heavily on embedded computing.

These systems typically run software known as firmware. Firmware is a type of software that is closely tied to the hardware it runs on. It is usually stored in non-volatile memory, allowing it to persist across power cycles. Depending on the complexity and requirements of the application, this firmware may operate on a bare-metal basis (without an operating system) or with the help of a real-time operating system (RTOS) that provides scheduling, task management, and interrupt handling capabilities.

One of the defining characteristics of embedded systems is determinism. The software running on these devices is expected to perform predictably and reliably under strict timing constraints. Missing a sensor reading or delaying an actuator response by even a few milliseconds can cause system failures or safety issues. Because of this, developers working on embedded systems must be highly aware of both the hardware behavior and the timing guarantees of their software.

Size and power consumption also play a critical role. Many embedded systems are deployed in environments where space is limited, or where they must operate on batteries for extended periods. This means the software must be efficient, avoiding unnecessary CPU usage, memory overhead, or power draw. Developers must be conscious of every byte and cycle, especially when working with 8-bit or 32-bit microcontrollers with very limited resources.

Embedded systems also tend to be isolated and reactive. They don't typically provide full user interfaces or network access like desktop systems. Instead, they react to external stimuli, such as sensor input, user button presses, or network messages. These events trigger specific behaviors encoded in the firmware. For example, a temperature sensor might trigger a fan if a threshold is exceeded, or a button press might toggle a relay controlling a motor.

Security, fault tolerance, and robustness are important design considerations. Many embedded devices run unattended in critical environments and may need to handle failures gracefully or recover after power loss. Firmware updates, either manually via USB or remotely over-the-air (OTA), must be secure and reliable to avoid rendering devices unusable.

In summary, an embedded system is a focused, efficient computing unit that serves a dedicated purpose in a constrained environment. It bridges software and hardware in a way that requires precision, safety, and reliability. Whether controlling a smart light bulb or managing a car's braking system, the role of an embedded system is to perform its function consistently and predictably with minimal resources. Understanding these constraints and requirements is essential for writing safe and efficient firmware—and that's exactly where Rust excels.

Common Challenges in Traditional Embedded Development

Developing software for embedded systems using traditional languages like C or C++ presents a number of challenges that are deeply tied to the nature of constrained hardware environments and the limitations of legacy toolchains. While these languages have served embedded developers for decades, they were never designed with modern software engineering safety and productivity in mind. As embedded systems grow more complex and expectations for reliability increase, these limitations become more pronounced.

One of the most fundamental issues in traditional embedded development is the lack of memory safety. In C, developers are given direct access to memory through raw pointers. This provides powerful control over how memory is used, but it also opens the door to serious bugs. If a pointer is not properly initialized, or if it references a region of memory that has already been freed, the result is undefined behavior. This could mean a crash, corrupted data, or subtle errors that appear only under specific timing conditions. Buffer overflows—where data is written past the end of an array—are especially dangerous and have led to countless security vulnerabilities and system failures.

Another critical challenge is managing concurrency in systems that rely on interrupts or real-time operating systems. Interrupts are hardware-triggered functions that allow a microcontroller to respond quickly to external events, such as a button press or incoming data on a serial line. While interrupts are essential in embedded applications, coordinating shared state between interrupt handlers and the main application logic can be error-prone. Traditional languages offer little protection against data races, where two pieces of code access shared memory at the same time in a way that causes unexpected behavior. Developers must use techniques like disabling interrupts, using volatile variables, or introducing critical sections—all of which require careful manual handling and can be difficult to get right consistently.

Limited debugging tools and runtime diagnostics add to the complexity. When something goes wrong on a microcontroller—perhaps a sensor stops responding or the system hangs unexpectedly—there is often no operating system to catch the error or provide logs. Developers must rely on hardware debuggers, serial output, or blinking LEDs to identify issues. Because of this, bugs that would be trivial to trace on a desktop system can take hours or even days to isolate and fix in an embedded environment.

Toolchain reliability is another area of concern. While desktop development benefits from mature compilers, package managers, and integrated build tools, traditional embedded development often involves manually managing toolchains, linker scripts, startup code, and hardware-specific configuration files. Cross-compilation, which is necessary to build code for a microcontroller from a PC, can be particularly fragile. Each vendor may provide its own development suite, often tightly coupled to proprietary IDEs and poorly documented libraries, making it hard to build portable or reusable code across hardware platforms.

Code reuse and abstraction in traditional embedded languages also tend to be limited. While object-oriented patterns are available in C++, they come with performance trade-offs and are often avoided in performance-critical applications. Developers trying to write portable drivers for sensors or displays must rely on preprocessor macros or function pointers, which lack the safety and flexibility of more modern abstraction mechanisms. This leads to duplicated code, configuration inconsistencies, and increased maintenance overhead.

Moreover, the lack of a modern package ecosystem can slow development. In embedded C, sharing and reusing code across projects typically involves copying source files, manually configuring build systems, and resolving hardware-specific differences by hand. There is no standard library in the conventional sense, and few tools offer built-in dependency resolution. As a result, even seasoned developers often end up building the same boilerplate components from scratch in project after project.

Finally, there is the issue of testing and verification. Embedded systems are notoriously difficult to test in isolation because their correctness often depends on hardware behavior. Unit testing frameworks are rare, and mocking hardware interactions is difficult without a strong type system or simulation environment. In many cases, the only real way to validate the behavior of firmware is to flash it to the hardware and observe its effect, which slows development and increases the risk of deploying unverified code.

All of these challenges lead to a development environment where small mistakes can have large consequences, and where safety, maintainability, and scalability are hard to achieve. As embedded devices are increasingly integrated into systems that require high reliability—such as medical instruments, industrial controllers, and connected consumer devices—the limitations of traditional languages become increasingly problematic.

This is why developers are beginning to look for alternatives that preserve the performance and control required by embedded systems while offering stronger safety guarantees and modern development tools. Rust has emerged as a compelling solution to these long-standing challenges by addressing many of them at the language level. Before we explore how Rust changes the game, it's important to understand just how much room there is for improvement—and how a better development model can lead to more robust, maintainable, and efficient embedded software.

Why Rust Is Ideal for Embedded Work

Rust is uniquely positioned to address many of the persistent challenges in embedded systems programming. It was designed from the ground up to offer both high performance and strong guarantees around memory safety and concurrency. These qualities make it particularly well-suited for low-level development tasks where correctness, efficiency, and control are critical.

One of Rust's most defining features is its ownership system, which ensures that memory is accessed in a safe and predictable way without needing a garbage collector. In traditional embedded development with C or C++, a significant portion of errors stem from manual memory management—using dangling pointers, leaking memory, or writing outside of allocated bounds. Rust's compiler enforces rules at compile time that prevent these issues. If code attempts to access freed memory or create two conflicting mutable references, the compiler refuses to build the program. This approach removes entire classes of bugs that would otherwise require careful auditing and runtime testing to detect.

In embedded systems, where software interacts directly with hardware, the ability to write code that is both safe and low-level is essential. Rust supports this through its powerful abstraction mechanisms. Traits, generics, and zero-cost abstractions allow developers to write reusable and flexible code that compiles down to highly efficient machine instructions. "Zero-cost" in this context means that abstraction does not come with a performance penalty. The compiler aggressively optimizes code, so abstractions like traits or iterators are typically inlined and compiled away. This makes it possible to write high-level logic while still operating within the strict constraints of embedded systems, such as limited memory or CPU cycles.

Concurrency is another area where Rust brings a significant advantage. Embedded systems frequently rely on interrupt-driven programming or real-time operating systems (RTOS) to handle concurrent tasks. This leads to shared state between different execution contexts, and managing that state safely can be difficult. Rust's type system is designed to prevent data races by default. It enforces rules about how memory can be shared and mutated across threads or tasks. In embedded contexts, this applies equally to shared resources accessed by both interrupt handlers and main application code. The compiler makes it clear when synchronization is needed, reducing the risk of subtle bugs that would otherwise only appear under rare timing conditions.

Rust's support for `no_std` development is another reason it fits well into embedded workflows. By default, most Rust programs link against the standard library (`std`), which depends on features like dynamic memory allocation and operating system services. However, in bare-metal embedded development, these features are not available. Rust allows developers to opt out of the standard library entirely and build applications using only the `core` library. This minimal runtime environment is designed specifically for platforms without an OS, and it enables developers to build efficient, predictable firmware with full control over the memory layout and hardware interaction.

The growing ecosystem around embedded Rust also contributes to its practicality. Libraries like `embedded-hal` define standard interfaces for hardware peripherals such as SPI, I2C, UART, and GPIO. This trait-based approach enables reusable drivers that can work across different microcontrollers. For example, a temperature sensor driver written using `embedded-hal` can be reused on an STM32, an nRF52, or an RP2040, provided the corresponding hardware abstraction layer (HAL) for the board implements the required traits. This modularity supports long-term maintainability and code reuse, two factors that have traditionally been difficult to achieve in embedded projects.

Tooling is another area where Rust stands out. The Rust compiler provides precise and readable error messages, helping developers understand what went wrong and how to fix it. The `cargo` build system and package manager simplify dependency management, cross-compilation, and reproducible builds. Tools like `probe-rs` and `defmt` extend this experience to embedded debugging by allowing firmware to be flashed and debugged over USB without relying on vendor-specific software. These tools make the development process more transparent, reliable, and modern compared to many legacy environments that rely on opaque IDEs and proprietary compilers.

Another important factor is code correctness and maintainability. Rust encourages developers to model program logic using types that encode invariants. For instance, hardware peripherals can be represented in code with types that change state as they are initialized, configured, and used. This technique, often referred to as the "type-state pattern," ensures that code cannot use a peripheral until it has been properly set up, and prevents misuse through static checks at compile time. The result is firmware that is more robust and easier to reason about.

Finally, Rust is supported by a strong and growing community of embedded developers. The Rust Embedded Working Group coordinates efforts to improve tooling, libraries, and documentation. There are also regularly updated device-specific crates, examples, and documentation to help new developers get started quickly. This level of community organization ensures that embedded Rust is not only usable today but is improving rapidly.

Taken together, Rust offers a powerful combination of safety, performance, and modern tooling that aligns well with the needs of embedded systems. It enables developers to write software that is safe by default, efficient without compromise, and scalable for complex applications. For anyone working in embedded systems who values correctness and long-term maintainability, Rust presents a compelling and practical option.

Overview of the Embedded Rust Ecosystem

The Embedded Rust ecosystem is a well-structured collection of tools, libraries, conventions, and community-driven efforts designed to support systems programming on resource-constrained hardware. It is built on the same foundations as the Rust programming language but tailored specifically for platforms that often lack an operating system, have limited memory, and require predictable real-time behavior. What makes this ecosystem particularly effective is its strong focus on safety, reusability, and hardware abstraction—combined with the ability to write highly efficient, low-level code.

At the core of this ecosystem is Rust's support for `no_std` development. In embedded systems, where there is no underlying operating system and often no dynamic memory allocation, the standard Rust library (`std`) cannot be used. Instead, embedded applications are written using the `core` library, a subset of the standard library that excludes OS-dependent functionality. This makes it possible to build firmware that runs directly on bare metal, without relying on system calls or dynamic memory features. The ability to opt into this minimal runtime gives embedded developers fine-grained control over every part of their program, from memory usage to interrupt behavior.

14

To support hardware-specific functionality, Rust developers make use of *Peripheral Access Crates* (PACs). These crates are automatically generated from SVD (System View Description) files provided by chip manufacturers. Each PAC maps directly to the memory-mapped registers of a specific microcontroller. This gives you safe, structured access to hardware features like timers, GPIO ports, serial interfaces, and ADCs (Analog-to-Digital Converters), all with strong typing and no unsafe pointer arithmetic. Rather than writing raw register addresses or macros, you work with clearly named methods and fields, which improves code clarity and reduces bugs.

Building on top of PACs are *Hardware Abstraction Layers* (HALs). A HAL provides a more user-friendly and device-agnostic interface to the hardware. While PACs expose the raw control registers, HALs wrap those details in safe, reusable APIs. This allows developers to write code that works across different chips without rewriting low-level logic. For example, toggling a GPIO pin or initializing an I2C peripheral looks the same whether you're using an STM32, an nRF microcontroller, or a RP2040—because the HAL implements standard traits that define consistent interfaces. These traits are part of the `embedded-hal` specification.

The `embedded-hal` crate defines a common set of traits for embedded drivers. Traits in Rust are like interfaces—they define method signatures without implementation. For example, the `OutputPin` trait defines methods like `set_high()` and `set_low()`, which can be implemented by any HAL that supports digital output. This abstraction enables a clean separation between device drivers and platform-specific code. A driver for a temperature sensor that uses SPI or I2C can be written generically to work with any microcontroller, as long as the platform's HAL supports the required traits. This separation improves portability, testability, and long-term maintainability.

Beyond basic peripheral access and abstraction, embedded Rust also supports real-time concurrency through frameworks like RTIC (Real-Time Interrupt-driven Concurrency). RTIC provides a structured way to write concurrent applications in Rust without a traditional RTOS. It allows developers to define tasks that run in response to interrupts, schedule execution with precise timing, and share resources safely using compile-time guarantees. Unlike traditional multitasking systems, RTIC focuses on determinism and static analysis, helping ensure that your code meets real-time requirements without runtime surprises.

For projects that benefit from asynchronous programming, `embassy` is another major component of the ecosystem. Embassy provides an async runtime specifically designed for embedded systems. It uses Rust's async/await syntax to express concurrent tasks in a readable way, while still meeting the constraints of systems without dynamic allocation or full operating system support. Embassy is well-suited for applications that involve a lot of waiting—such as handling sensors, timers, or network interfaces—without blocking the CPU.

Debugging is a major part of any embedded workflow, and Rust offers modern tools in this area as well. The `defmt` logging framework provides efficient and compact debug output, suitable even for low-resource microcontrollers. When paired with `probe-rs`, a cross-platform tool for flashing and debugging embedded devices, developers can view logs, set breakpoints, and step through code—all without needing vendor-specific IDEs or proprietary tools. These tools are designed to integrate seamlessly with Rust's workflow and emphasize ease of use and transparency.

The build process in embedded Rust is handled by `cargo`, Rust's package manager and build system. Cargo makes it easy to manage dependencies, compile for specific targets, and organize your project structure. For embedded work, it supports cross-compilation through the use of target specifications. Developers can define which architecture they are building for (such as `thumbv7em-none-eabihf` for ARM Cortex-M microcontrollers), and cargo handles the rest, producing firmware ready to be flashed to a device.

All of these tools and libraries are supported by a vibrant and well-organized community. The Rust Embedded Working Group coordinates development across the ecosystem, curates resources, and ensures that the tools evolve together in a coherent way. Community projects, device-specific crates, HAL implementations, and learning resources are all maintained in open repositories with active contributors. This level of collaboration makes it easier for new developers to get started and for experienced developers to contribute back.

In essence, the embedded Rust ecosystem provides the infrastructure necessary to write safe, reusable, and high-performance firmware across a wide range of hardware platforms. With strong abstractions, modern tooling, and a growing library of community-supported components, Rust allows embedded developers to focus on building reliable systems without sacrificing control or performance. As the ecosystem continues to mature, it is becoming not just a viable option, but a highly competitive one for professional embedded development.

Chapter 2: Getting Started with Embedded Rust Development

Before we can begin writing firmware in Rust for embedded systems, we need to set up a solid development environment. This means installing the necessary toolchain, configuring our build system for cross-compilation, choosing appropriate hardware, and finally writing and flashing a basic program to confirm everything is working.

In this chapter, we'll walk through each of these steps with care. Whether you're new to embedded development or just transitioning to Rust from C, the goal is to help you feel confident and in control of your setup from day one.

Installing the Rust Toolchain and Target Support

Before you can write your first embedded Rust application, you need to prepare your development environment by installing the appropriate toolchain and configuring your system for cross-compilation. In embedded development, the software you write on your computer is compiled to run on a completely different processor architecture—typically a microcontroller using the ARM Cortex-M series. This requires configuring Rust to produce binaries for the microcontroller instead of your own machine.

The starting point is installing Rust itself. Fortunately, Rust has a unified installer and version manager called `rustup`, which simplifies this process. `rustup` lets you install multiple versions of Rust, update them easily, and switch between toolchains with minimal effort. It also handles installing additional components like target architectures and build tools.

To install Rust, you should use your terminal or command prompt. On any major operating system, run the official installation script:

```
curl --proto '=https' --tlsv1.2 -sSf
https://sh.rustup.rs | sh
```

This command downloads and launches the Rust installer. It guides you through the installation interactively, setting up everything you need to compile Rust applications on your local system. Once the installation is complete, you should verify that `rustc` (the compiler) and `cargo` (Rust's build tool and package manager) are available by running:

```
rustc --version
```

```
cargo --version
```

These commands confirm that Rust is now accessible from your terminal. From here, you can compile and manage Rust projects just like you would for any native application. However, for embedded development, your goal is not to compile for your desktop environment (typically x86_64) but for your target microcontroller—usually an ARM-based chip.

Cross-compilation is the process of compiling code on one architecture (your PC) to run on another (the microcontroller). Rust supports this out of the box through the use of *targets*, which describe the architecture, instruction set, and ABI of the output binary.

You'll need to add support for your target microcontroller. For most ARM Cortex-M processors, the appropriate target name starts with `thumb`, referring to the Thumb instruction set used by ARM for reduced-size instructions.

For example, if you're targeting a Cortex-M4 or Cortex-M7 chip with hardware floating-point support (a common choice in modern development boards), the Rust target is:

```
thumbv7em-none-eabihf
```

This name breaks down as follows:

`thumbv7em`: Specifies the ARMv7E-M architecture (used by Cortex-M4 and M7).

`none`: Indicates that there is no operating system—this is bare-metal programming.

`eabihf`: Refers to the Embedded ABI with hardware floating-point support.

You can add this target using `rustup`:

```
rustup target add thumbv7em-none-eabihf
```

If you are using a Cortex-M0 or M0+ device, such as the RP2040 on the Raspberry Pi Pico, the appropriate target might be:

thumbv6m-none-eabi

In that case, you'd run:

```
rustup target add thumbv6m-none-eabi
```

Adding a target is not enough on its own—you also need to ensure that your code can be compiled and linked properly. This means providing a linker script that defines the memory layout of the target microcontroller and installing binary utilities like `objcopy` or `ld`. These tools help convert Rust's compiled binaries into the formats required by microcontrollers (typically `.bin` or `.elf` files).

You can install the required binary utilities using the following command:

```
cargo install cargo-binutils
```

```
rustup component add llvm-tools-preview
```

This will give you access to commands like `cargo objcopy`, which lets you convert your compiled Rust programs into the correct format for flashing onto a board.

At this point, your Rust toolchain is capable of producing code for the target microcontroller, but the compiler still needs to know which target to use when building a specific project. You can tell `cargo` to build for the embedded target by specifying it explicitly in the build command:

```
cargo build --target=thumbv7em-none-eabihf
```

Or, to avoid specifying it every time, you can create a configuration file inside your project directory. In `.cargo/config.toml`, write:

```
[build]

target = "thumbv7em-none-eabihf"
```

This makes cross-compilation the default for that project, ensuring that all builds are automatically configured for the embedded target.

With this setup, you're able to write Rust programs on your development machine and compile them for ARM Cortex-M microcontrollers. This is the foundation you'll build on in future chapters, where you'll add board support crates, configure your project for bare-metal execution, and write real firmware that interacts with hardware.

To test that everything works, you can create a new minimal library crate and try building it for your target:

```
cargo new --lib embedded_test

cd embedded_test

cargo build

cargo build --target=thumbv7em-none-eabihf
```

If the build completes successfully, your toolchain is configured correctly. You now have the ability to cross-compile Rust code for embedded platforms—one of the most critical steps in developing safe, reliable firmware using modern tooling. In the next section, we'll look at setting up the rest of your environment, including flashing tools and debug support, so you can run your code on real hardware.

Setting Up Your Development Environment

Once your Rust toolchain is installed and your embedded target support is configured, the next step is setting up your development environment to allow you to write, build, flash, and debug firmware with ease and confidence. A well-prepared environment reduces friction during development, improves your feedback loop, and helps you diagnose and solve issues quickly. The setup includes both software tools on your computer and the hardware connection to your microcontroller board.

Let's start with the build and flashing tools that will allow you to work with embedded targets efficiently. While Rust's default build tool `cargo` is already powerful, embedded development introduces additional requirements. You need to compile for a non-native target, convert the output binary to the correct format, flash it onto the board, and often observe debug output or logs over a hardware interface.

To enable these workflows, you'll want to install `cargo-binutils`, a collection of helper commands that integrate with `cargo` and give you access to utilities like `objdump`, `objcopy`, and `size`. These tools allow you to analyze and prepare your firmware binary for deployment.

You can install these utilities by running:

```
cargo install cargo-binutils

rustup component add llvm-tools-preview
```

This command enables support for LLVM-based tools and allows you to do things like convert your `.elf` file into a `.bin` or `.hex` file suitable for flashing to your microcontroller's flash memory. A common conversion looks like this:

```
cargo objcopy --release -- -O binary
target/thumbv7em-none-
eabihf/release/your_project.bin
```

You will also need a flashing tool that can communicate with your target board over a debug probe. One of the most flexible tools available today is `probe-rs`. Unlike many vendor-specific flashing tools, `probe-rs` is open source, written in Rust, and supports a wide range of ARM Cortex-M microcontrollers and debug probes.

You can install the `probe-rs` command-line utility by running:

```
cargo install probe-rs-cli
```

After installation, you can flash your firmware using a command like:

```
probe-rs-cli run --chip STM32F303VCT6
target/thumbv7em-none-eabihf/release/your_project
```

Make sure to replace `STM32F303VCT6` with the name of your actual chip. You'll find the correct name in your microcontroller's datasheet or on the manufacturer's website. The `probe-rs` tool detects the connected debugger and communicates with the target device over USB.

To simplify flashing, logging, and debugging, you can also install `cargo-embed`. It wraps many of the features of `probe-rs` into a convenient workflow tool tailored specifically for embedded Rust development.

Install it with:

```
cargo install cargo-embed
```

To use `cargo-embed`, create a file called `Embed.toml` in your project root. This configuration file tells the tool which chip you're targeting and how to behave during flashing and logging:

```
[default]

chip = "STM32F303VCT6"

log_level = "info"
```

With this in place, you can flash and start logging output with:

```
cargo embed
```

This command will compile your project for the specified target, flash it to the board, and start reading logs over RTT (Real-Time Transfer), which is a fast and efficient protocol for reading debug output from the microcontroller.

For logging to work efficiently on embedded targets, especially where UART output may not be available or practical, the `defmt` framework is a great option. It provides compact logging macros specifically optimized for embedded systems. To use `defmt`, you'll need a logger like `defmt-rtt` and a panic handler such as `defmt-panic`.

Here's how you would configure your dependencies in `Cargo.toml`:

```
[dependencies]

defmt = "0.3"

defmt-rtt = "0.4"

defmt-panic = "0.3"
```

In your `main.rs`, you can now add logging statements like:

```
defmt::info!("System initialized.");
```

These messages will be visible in your terminal when using `cargo embed`.

In terms of the development editor, Visual Studio Code (VS Code) is a great choice for embedded Rust. It supports the Rust Language Server (`rust-analyzer`), integrates well with embedded workflows, and provides excellent syntax highlighting, inlay hints, code navigation, and error checking. Install the "rust-analyzer" extension and configure it to use your project's target specification. You can also install "CodeLLDB" for debugging support when connected to your target hardware.

To further streamline your development workflow, you may want to add a `.vscode/launch.json` file to configure debugging for embedded targets using `probe-rs-debugger` or GDB-compatible interfaces.

Finally, don't forget to ensure that udev rules are properly configured on Linux to allow access to your debug probe without requiring `sudo`. Vendors often supply these rules in their toolchain packages or documentation. On Windows, most popular probes work via USB with drivers like WinUSB or through vendor-specific drivers like ST-Link or SEGGER's J-Link.

Once your environment is configured, your firmware development process becomes smooth and repeatable: you write Rust code, compile for the target, flash using `cargo-embed`, and monitor output using RTT or serial logs. You can step through code, set breakpoints, and inspect memory, all using safe and modern tooling.

Setting up a robust embedded Rust environment is not just about installing tools—it's about creating a development process where feedback is fast, errors are caught early, and confidence grows with each successful build. With this foundation in place, you're ready to begin developing real embedded applications that interact with hardware using the full power of Rust's safety and performance.

Choosing a Microcontroller Board

Selecting the right microcontroller board is one of the most important early decisions you'll make in your embedded Rust development journey. The board you choose determines what peripherals are available, what hardware abstractions you'll work with, which drivers you'll need, and ultimately, how productive you'll be as you learn and build real-world applications. The good news is that the Rust embedded ecosystem has grown significantly, and there are now many microcontroller boards that are well supported with high-quality libraries and documentation.

When evaluating a board for embedded Rust development, there are a few practical criteria you should keep in mind. First and foremost is hardware support. Rust's ecosystem provides board-specific crates, called **Board Support Crates (BSPs)**, which are built on top of the **Hardware Abstraction Layer (HAL)** for that board's microcontroller family. You want to choose a board for which a BSP and a HAL already exist and are actively maintained. Without this support, you would have to write a lot of boilerplate code to initialize peripherals and interact with hardware registers directly.

Let's go through what makes a board Rust-friendly and practical for your learning and prototyping.

Look for a board that has an onboard **debug probe**, such as a CMSIS-DAP, ST-Link, or SEGGER J-Link interface. This is essential for flashing firmware, debugging code, and logging runtime output. When this feature is built-in, it removes the need to purchase and connect an external debugger. For example, the STM32F3 Discovery board includes an onboard ST-Link debugger that works seamlessly with `probe-rs` and `cargo-embed`, making it an excellent candidate for testing embedded Rust code.

You should also consider how accessible the GPIO pins are and whether there are LEDs, buttons, or simple peripherals already wired up to the microcontroller. Having a user-controllable LED or a testable button makes it much easier to verify that your code is working as expected. For example, if you're writing a simple "blinky" program to toggle an LED, you'll want that LED to be connected to a known GPIO pin—and ideally, documented in the BSP for that board.

Memory size is another factor. Embedded Rust does not use a garbage collector, but the compiler and build tools still have a memory footprint. Boards with at least 32 KB of RAM and 128 KB of flash are a comfortable starting point, especially if you plan to use logging via RTT or explore concurrency features using frameworks like RTIC or Embassy.

The Raspberry Pi Pico is a great example of a well-supported, cost-effective board for beginners. It features the RP2040 microcontroller, which uses a dual-core ARM Cortex-M0+ and offers a substantial set of peripherals including GPIO, SPI, I2C, UART, and USB. The Rust community has created a BSP for the Pico, as well as a complete HAL for the RP2040 chip family. It also supports flashing via USB using a UF2 bootloader, so you don't even need a dedicated debug probe to get started.

If your goal is to build wireless applications—such as Bluetooth or LoRa—you might prefer a board like the nRF52840-DK. It uses a Nordic microcontroller with integrated Bluetooth Low Energy support, and its HAL and BSP are mature and maintained by the community. With support for CMSIS-DAP debugging and peripherals like buttons and LEDs onboard, it's ready for more advanced experiments.

Once you've narrowed down a board that suits your development goals and has strong Rust support, you should install the relevant crates. For example, for the STM32F3 Discovery board, you'd use:

```
[dependencies.stm32f3xx-hal]

version = "0.9"

features = ["stm32f303", "rt"]
```

This tells `cargo` to pull in the HAL for the STM32F3 family and include runtime support. The `rt` feature ensures that startup and interrupt vector definitions are included via the `cortex-m-rt` crate.

For the Raspberry Pi Pico:

```
[dependencies.rp-pico]

version = "0.8"
```

This includes both the HAL and the board-specific configuration that makes it easier to work with the LED, buttons, and USB interface on the Pico.

Once you've selected and connected your board, the next step is to confirm that it is recognized by your development tools. Connect it via USB, then run:

```
probe-rs-cli list
```

This should output the name and identifier of your connected microcontroller. If it does, your board is successfully communicating with the toolchain. If not, check that your udev rules (on Linux) or drivers (on Windows) are correctly installed for your board's debug interface.

At this point, you're ready to write your first firmware project and flash it onto real hardware. Choosing the right board gives you the ability to explore the features of embedded Rust in a supportive, frictionless environment. A good board enables rapid prototyping, reliable debugging, and exposure to real peripherals—setting the stage for productive and professional embedded systems development.

Building and Flashing Your First Bare-Metal Rust Program

With your Rust toolchain installed, your development environment configured, and a supported microcontroller board connected, you're now ready to build and flash your first bare-metal Rust program. This is a crucial step—not just to verify that everything is set up correctly, but also to help you understand how Rust interacts with hardware when there is no operating system involved.

In this section, you'll build a simple program that toggles an LED on your microcontroller board. This might seem basic, but it's an essential milestone that confirms the complete flow: writing code, compiling for an embedded target, flashing it onto the board, and observing real hardware behavior.

To begin, you'll create a new Rust project. Use the `--bin` flag to generate a binary crate:

```
cargo new blinky --bin

cd blinky
```

Then, configure the project for bare-metal development. In `Cargo.toml`, you need to specify that your project won't use Rust's standard library. Instead, it will rely on the `core` crate, which provides only low-level functionality suited for constrained environments.

Update your `Cargo.toml` as follows:

```
[package]
name = "blinky"
version = "0.1.0"
edition = "2021"

[dependencies]
cortex-m = "0.7"
cortex-m-rt = "0.7"
panic-halt = "0.2"

[dependencies.stm32f3xx-hal]
version = "0.9"
features = ["stm32f303", "rt"]
```

This example uses the STM32F3 Discovery board. If you're working with another board, replace the HAL crate and features accordingly. The `panic-halt` crate defines a panic handler that simply halts the processor on panic, which is a safe behavior for early-stage firmware.

Next, create a `.cargo/config.toml` file to tell `cargo` which target you're compiling for:

```
[build]

target = "thumbv7em-none-eabihf"
```

You also need a `memory.x` linker script, which tells the compiler where the flash and RAM are located on your microcontroller. For many boards, the BSP or HAL will provide a default `memory.x` file, or you can copy it from an example project. For the STM32F303VCT6, your linker script might look like this:

```
MEMORY
{
  FLASH : ORIGIN = 0x08000000, LENGTH = 256K
  RAM   : ORIGIN = 0x20000000, LENGTH = 40K
}
```

Save this as `memory.x` in your project root and make sure to tell Cargo about it in your `Cargo.toml`:

```
[package.metadata.cortex-m-rt]
```

```
memory-x = "memory.x"
```

Now, you're ready to write your firmware. In `src/main.rs`, start with the following structure:

```
#![no_std]
#![no_main]

use cortex_m_rt::entry;
use panic_halt as _;

use stm32f3xx_hal as hal;
use hal::prelude::*;
use hal::pac;

#[entry]
fn main() -> ! {
    // Take ownership of the device peripherals
    let dp = pac::Peripherals::take().unwrap();

    // Set up the clock configuration
    let mut rcc = dp.RCC.constrain();
    let mut gpioe = dp.GPIOE.split(&mut rcc.ahb);

    // Configure pin PE9 as push-pull output (this
is the onboard LED on STM32F3 Discovery)
    let mut led =
gpioe.pe9.into_push_pull_output(&mut gpioe.moder,
&mut gpioe.otyper);

    loop {
        led.toggle().ok();
        cortex_m::asm::delay(8_000_000);
    }
}
```

This code does several important things:

It sets the crate to run without the standard library (`#![no_std]`) and without a main function in the usual sense (`#![no_main]`). Instead, it uses the `#[entry]` attribute to define the firmware's entry point.

It initializes the microcontroller's peripherals using the PAC (Peripheral Access Crate).

It configures the RCC (reset and clock control) and the GPIOE port.

It sets the PE9 pin (which is connected to an onboard LED) as an output.

It enters a loop where the LED is toggled, and a delay is added using a busy-wait.

To compile your project, use the standard `cargo build` command:

```
cargo build --release
```

This generates the firmware binary in the `target/thumbv7em-none-eabihf/release` directory. You can inspect the size of your binary or convert it into a raw binary format using `cargo objcopy` if needed:

```
cargo objcopy --release -- -O binary blinky.bin
```

To flash the firmware onto your board, use `cargo-embed` or `probe-rs-cli`. If you've configured `Embed.toml` already with your chip's name, flashing becomes straightforward:

```
cargo embed
```

If you're using `probe-rs-cli` directly, the flashing command looks like this:

```
probe-rs-cli run --chip STM32F303VCT6
target/thumbv7em-none-eabihf/release/blinky
```

Once the flashing process completes successfully, the LED on your board should begin blinking at regular intervals. That single blinking LED is proof that everything is working—your code compiled correctly, your toolchain produced valid machine code for the target, your debug probe successfully communicated with the board, and your Rust firmware is running on real hardware.

This program is deliberately minimal, but it reflects the core process of embedded development with Rust: write expressive code using safe abstractions, compile it for a bare-metal target, flash it with reliable tools, and verify functionality directly on hardware.

Now that you've completed the full loop from code to hardware, you're in a strong position to begin experimenting with other peripherals, interrupts, timers, and communication protocols. You've just taken your first real step into efficient, safe, and modern embedded systems development.

Chapter 3: `no_std` and Rust for Resource-Constrained Devices

When writing embedded applications in Rust, one of the first concepts you'll encounter is `no_std`. This is not just a configuration detail—it represents a shift in how we think about software in environments where there is no operating system, no dynamic memory allocation, and no room for runtime surprises. Embedded systems are often constrained by strict limitations on memory, performance, and power usage. In these settings, writing lean, deterministic code isn't just an optimization—it's a necessity.

What `no_std` Means and Why It Matters

In embedded systems development, particularly when you're working directly with microcontrollers, there's no underlying operating system to rely on. There's no filesystem, no system-provided memory allocator, no standard input/output streams, and often no way to run multithreaded tasks in the conventional sense. The kind of programming you're doing is bare-metal—your code is the only thing running on the processor, and it's expected to be minimal, efficient, and fully in control of the hardware. In this environment, you need a programming model that's optimized for direct hardware interaction with complete predictability. That's exactly where `no_std` comes into play in Rust.

By default, Rust programs are linked against the standard library (`std`). This library is designed to provide all the usual conveniences of a modern programming language—things like file access, networking, dynamic memory allocation, threading, and more. However, those features depend heavily on operating system services. In embedded systems, where such services are absent, trying to use `std` simply doesn't make sense. This is why embedded Rust uses `#![no_std]`—an attribute that tells the compiler not to link against the standard library.

Instead, `no_std` programs rely on the `core` library. The `core` crate is a lightweight subset of the standard library that provides the building blocks of the Rust language: primitive types (`u8`, `i32`, etc.), traits like `Copy`, `Clone`, and `Iterator`, and operations on arrays, slices, options, and results. These features

32

are implemented without assuming the presence of an operating system or dynamic memory.

To use `no_std`, you start every embedded application with this attribute:

`#![no_std]`

This line must appear at the top of your crate's main source file. It tells the compiler that your program won't use the standard library and that you, the developer, will take full responsibility for things like panic handling and program startup.

Let's look at a minimal example:

```
#![no_std]
#![no_main]

use cortex_m_rt::entry;
use panic_halt as _;

#[entry]
fn main() -> ! {
    loop {
        // Your embedded code runs here
    }
}
```

This is a bare-metal embedded Rust program. It has no access to `println!`, `Vec`, or any of the standard library types that require dynamic memory or I/O. It does, however, have access to all the core language features and can run on the smallest microcontrollers with as little as 16 KB of flash and 4 KB of RAM.

The lack of `std` isn't a limitation—it's a feature. Without dynamic memory allocation, there are no heap-related bugs like fragmentation, double free, or use-after-free. Without threads, you avoid data races and synchronization bugs. Everything in your code happens in a single, predictable execution context (unless you explicitly introduce interrupts or real-time scheduling). These properties are crucial in real-time and safety-critical systems, where deterministic behavior is essential.

Of course, there are trade-offs. Without `std`, you give up access to convenient types like `String`, `Vec`, and `HashMap` unless you reimplement them in a heapless fashion. Fortunately, the Rust ecosystem provides alternatives through crates like heapless and arrayvec. These crates provide versions of these data structures that operate on fixed-size buffers.

For example, if you need a dynamically sized buffer but can't use `Vec` because it requires a heap, you can use `heapless::Vec`:

```
use heapless::Vec;

let mut buffer: Vec<u8, 32> = Vec::new();
buffer.push(42).unwrap();
```

This `Vec` is backed by a fixed-size array of 32 bytes. It behaves like a dynamic vector within those limits, but it never allocates memory on the heap, and its size and behavior are fully deterministic.

Logging is another area where `no_std` impacts your workflow. Without access to `std::println!`, you need to rely on platform-specific logging mechanisms. In embedded Rust, this is often done using RTT (Real-Time Transfer) with the `defmt` crate, or via UART-based serial output. These logging systems are designed to be efficient and safe for use in low-resource environments.

To handle panics in `no_std` environments, you must provide your own panic behavior. One common approach is to halt the processor, using the `panic-halt` crate:

```
use panic_halt as _;
```

When a panic occurs, this crate simply disables interrupts and enters an infinite loop. This is usually enough for basic applications or for use during early development. In more advanced systems, you might log the panic reason over RTT, blink an error code using LEDs, or trigger a watchdog reset.

Another important feature in `no_std` development is the startup process. Without an operating system, your application is responsible for configuring the stack, initializing data segments, and jumping to your `main` function. Rust's `cortex-m-rt` crate handles these details for ARM Cortex-M devices.

It provides a default reset handler and interrupt vector table, allowing you to focus on writing your application logic.

The typical embedded startup function looks like this:

```
#[entry]
fn main() -> ! {
    // Initialization code here
    loop {
        // Main loop
    }
}
```

The `#[entry]` attribute comes from `cortex-m-rt` and replaces the usual `fn main()` entry point. It ensures that your application starts at the right place after the device powers on or resets.

When you're using `no_std`, every byte of code and data is there because you explicitly put it there or opted into it through a crate. This results in extremely compact binaries and tight control over memory usage—something that is critical when working with devices that have only a few kilobytes of RAM or flash.

By using `no_std`, you also gain portability. Because your code doesn't depend on an operating system, you can move it between platforms with minimal changes. Whether you're running on an STM32, an nRF52, or a RISC-V microcontroller, your Rust code can remain nearly identical—provided the HAL layer supports the hardware.

no_std is not just a technical configuration—it's the foundation of writing safe, portable, and efficient embedded applications in Rust. It strips away assumptions about the runtime environment and gives you full control over what your firmware does and how it does it. And with the powerful abstractions Rust offers, working in `no_std` doesn't mean you have to sacrifice expressiveness or safety. Instead, it allows you to build small, correct, and composable embedded software that runs predictably and reliably on even the most constrained devices.

Static Memory and Heap-Free Programming

In embedded systems, everything revolves around predictability and efficiency. There are no operating system services, and in most cases, there is no memory management unit (MMU) to support dynamic memory allocation. This means you cannot rely on a heap for runtime allocation of memory. Instead, your code must operate using a fixed, pre-determined amount of memory, and you must know where and how every variable lives in memory—before the device even starts executing your firmware.

Rust's design makes this kind of programming not just possible but safe and ergonomic. The language encourages the use of static memory and stack allocation by default. Even though heap allocation is available in general-purpose Rust through types like Box, Vec, and String, these are off-limits in no_std environments unless you explicitly bring in an allocator, which is usually avoided in microcontroller-based firmware. As a result, you'll need to develop your applications using static and stack-based memory structures, which Rust is extremely well-suited for.

Let's clarify what static memory means in this context. When you declare a variable as static, that value is allocated at a fixed memory address for the entire lifetime of the program. It does not live on the stack, and it does not get freed. It's always there—just like the flash memory where your firmware lives. Here's a basic example:

```
static mut BUFFER: [u8; 256] = [0; 256];
```

This line creates a 256-byte buffer that exists in RAM from the moment your program starts. It doesn't need to be dynamically allocated, and it won't be deallocated. However, static mut introduces potential for unsafe access because this buffer can be modified from anywhere at any time. To access it, Rust requires an unsafe block:

```
unsafe {
    BUFFER[0] = 1;
}
```

Using unsafe isn't inherently bad, but it signals to you and to the compiler that you're bypassing some of Rust's safety guarantees. That's why in most embedded Rust applications, it's better to pass memory around through functions, structures, or safe abstractions where ownership and borrowing rules still apply.

Most embedded Rust code operates primarily using **stack allocation**. When you declare a variable inside a function, it lives on the stack and disappears when that function exits. This is safe and efficient for short-lived data. Here's an example of a buffer that exists only during the function's execution:

```
fn handle_data() {
    let mut buffer: [u8; 128] = [0; 128];
    buffer[0] = 42;
}
```

Because this buffer lives on the stack, it uses memory only temporarily, and the compiler ensures that it's automatically cleaned up when `handle_data` returns. Stack allocation works beautifully for intermediate data structures, temporary I/O buffers, and function-local computations.

But sometimes you need more flexibility—structures that behave like heap-allocated containers, but without the heap. That's where crates like `heapless` come in. `heapless` offers data structures like `Vec`, `String`, `RingBuffer`, and `LinearMap` that work without dynamic memory allocation. Instead, they use fixed-capacity backing storage, defined at compile time.

Here's an example using a fixed-capacity vector:

```
use heapless::Vec;

fn log_sensor_values() {
    let mut values: Vec<u16, 16> = Vec::new();

    for i in 0..10 {
        values.push(i * 10).unwrap();
    }

    // values now contains: [0, 10, 20, ..., 90]
}
```

This vector is backed by a static buffer of 16 elements. It behaves like a dynamic vector, but it never allocates memory at runtime. Instead, all the memory it might need is reserved ahead of time. This kind of structure is invaluable in embedded Rust because it lets you work with flexible data while maintaining full control over memory usage.

Another useful pattern is passing buffers into functions so they can be reused without needing new allocations. Here's a simple pattern for reusing a buffer across function calls:

```
fn fill_buffer(buf: &mut [u8]) {
    for (i, byte) in buf.iter_mut().enumerate() {
        *byte = (i % 256) as u8;
    }
}

fn main() -> ! {
    let mut buffer: [u8; 64] = [0; 64];
    fill_buffer(&mut buffer);

    loop {
        // use buffer for something, like sending
over UART
    }
}
```

In this example, no heap is involved, and the function doesn't return a new buffer—it fills the existing one. This approach reduces memory overhead and ensures your application is always working within known constraints.

Sometimes you'll want data to live beyond the lifetime of a function. If you can't use `static`, the best approach is often to move ownership of the data up to a larger scope. In Rust, this might mean storing the data inside a struct or wrapping it in a safe global singleton, often managed through crates like `cortex-m::singleton`, which allows one-time static initialization without unsafe code.

Here's a practical example using `singleton!` to create a shared buffer that lives for the entire program duration:

```
use cortex_m::singleton;

fn main() -> ! {
    let buffer: &'static mut [u8; 128] =
singleton!(: [u8; 128] = [0; 128]).unwrap();
```

```
    buffer[0] = 1;

    loop {
        // Use the buffer here safely
    }
}
```

This macro ensures that only one such buffer can exist, and it returns a safe mutable reference that you can use throughout your program. It's a great way to have long-lived, globally accessible data without stepping into unsafe territory.

In embedded systems, knowing the exact memory layout of your application is a major advantage. With no_std, static, and stack-allocated memory patterns, you are always in control. You can check memory usage during compilation using tools like cargo size or by examining the .map file produced by your linker. This level of visibility allows you to write firmware that is efficient and robust—even on microcontrollers with very limited resources.

Working without a heap may sound restrictive, but it actually encourages better software design. You're forced to think about the lifetime of every piece of data. You design your systems with known capacities and predictable behavior. There are no surprises at runtime because every allocation, every access, and every buffer is explicitly accounted for.

Rust's language features and its ecosystem make this kind of development approachable and safe. You can write expressive, reusable code that meets the demands of embedded systems—without compromising on control, reliability, or performance.

Ownership and Borrowing in Embedded Contexts

Ownership and borrowing are at the core of how Rust ensures memory safety without a garbage collector. These concepts help you reason clearly about who owns what, who can access it, and when access is allowed or denied. While they apply universally across all Rust code, they are especially powerful in embedded systems—where safety, predictability, and control over memory access are critical.

In embedded development, you work close to the hardware. You're manipulating registers, configuring peripherals, managing global resources like clocks, timers, and buses. If two parts of your firmware try to access the same peripheral at the same time—say, one from the main loop and another from an interrupt—you can easily end up with subtle, hard-to-trace bugs. Rust's ownership model exists specifically to prevent these kinds of errors, and it does so in a way that is checked entirely at compile time.

Ownership in Embedded Applications

Ownership in Rust means that each value in the program has a single place in the code that is responsible for it. When that value is passed to a function or a variable, ownership moves. If a peripheral, buffer, or hardware register block is owned by one part of your code, it cannot be used elsewhere unless ownership is explicitly transferred.

In embedded systems, this model gives you strong guarantees. For instance, when you take control of your microcontroller's hardware registers using `pac::Peripherals::take()`, you gain exclusive access to all the peripheral register blocks:

```
let peripherals =
pac::Peripherals::take().unwrap();
```

This method can only be called once. After that, if you try to call it again, it returns `None`. This is Rust enforcing that there can be only one owner of the peripheral access—exactly what you want when dealing with hardware that should not be accessed concurrently.

Once you have access to the peripheral struct, you usually hand parts of it off to hardware abstraction layers (HALs). For example, you might pass the GPIO block to configure pins:

```
let mut rcc = peripherals.RCC.constrain();
let mut gpioe = peripherals.GPIOE.split(&mut
rcc.ahb);
let mut led = gpioe.pe9.into_push_pull_output(&mut
gpioe.moder, &mut gpioe.otyper);
```

40

In this code, each call consumes part of the peripheral tree and hands ownership to the HAL's internal configuration code. This design ensures that once a GPIO pin is configured as an output, no part of the code can reconfigure it unless you still hold the appropriate configuration state. It eliminates entire classes of bugs where a pin might be used in the wrong mode or reinitialized midway through execution.

Borrowing and Lifetimes

Sometimes, you don't want to take full ownership of a value—you just want to temporarily access it. That's where borrowing comes in. In Rust, you can borrow something immutably (`&T`) or mutably (`&mut T`), but not both at the same time.

This is critical in embedded contexts. Suppose you have a shared buffer you want to modify:

```
fn fill_buffer(buf: &mut [u8]) {
    for i in 0..buf.len() {
        buf[i] = i as u8;
    }
}
```

The function takes a mutable borrow of the buffer and fills it. You cannot use the buffer elsewhere while this function is running because only one mutable reference can exist at a time. This prevents race conditions and unexpected mutations.

Now, suppose you want to split a peripheral and access different parts of it. Many HALs are designed with this use case in mind. When you call `split()` on a GPIO block, it gives you multiple objects, each owning a single pin. This means you can use pins independently, without worrying that modifying one affects another.

Here's a real-world example using two output pins:

```
let mut gpioc = dp.GPIOC.split(&mut rcc.ahb);

let mut led1 = gpioc.pc8.into_push_pull_output(&mut
gpioc.moder, &mut gpioc.otyper);
```

```
let mut led2 = gpioc.pc9.into_push_pull_output(&mut
gpioc.moder, &mut gpioc.otyper);

led1.set_high().unwrap();
led2.set_low().unwrap();
```

Each pin is a separate object with its own ownership. The HAL ensures that once you've configured a pin, it cannot be reconfigured accidentally from another part of the program. Ownership makes this guarantee possible.

Shared Access and Interrupts

In embedded systems, interrupts are a common source of concurrency. When an interrupt fires, it might want to read from or write to a shared buffer. But the main application might also be using that buffer at the same time. If you're not careful, this can lead to race conditions.

Rust forces you to deal with this explicitly. If you're sharing a buffer between your main loop and an interrupt, you must use synchronization mechanisms to ensure safe access. For Cortex-M targets, this typically involves critical sections or atomic operations.

Here's a simplified example using the `cortex-m` crate's `interrupt::free()` function:

```
static mut SHARED_COUNTER: u32 = 0;

fn increment() {
    cortex_m::interrupt::free(|_cs| {
        unsafe {
            SHARED_COUNTER += 1;
        }
    });
}
```

This code temporarily disables interrupts to ensure that no other context modifies SHARED_COUNTER while it's being updated. This pattern is a safe way to access static mut data without causing data races. In production systems, more robust solutions like the `critical-section` crate or RTIC (Real-Time Interrupt-driven Concurrency) framework should be used to manage shared state with compile-time checks.

Ownership Across State Transitions

Embedded applications often go through state transitions. A peripheral starts in an unconfigured state, then it's configured, then it's used, and eventually might be disabled. Rust encourages you to model each of these states explicitly through types.

This pattern is called the **type-state pattern**. You define distinct types for each configuration state, and the compiler ensures that only valid transitions are possible.

Here's an example of what that might look like in simplified form:

```rust
struct UninitializedUart;
struct ConfiguredUart;

impl UninitializedUart {
    fn configure(self, baudrate: u32) ->
ConfiguredUart {
        // Perform setup
        ConfiguredUart
    }
}

impl ConfiguredUart {
    fn write(&self, byte: u8) {
        // Send byte over UART
    }
}
```

With this pattern, code cannot call `write()` unless the UART is properly configured. If someone tries to skip the `configure()` step, the code simply won't compile. This use of ownership and type modeling eliminates bugs at build time that would be difficult to catch during testing.

Rust's ownership and borrowing system gives embedded developers tools they've always needed: the ability to express exclusive access, safe sharing, and correct sequencing of operations—without relying on conventions or comments.

It transforms the way you reason about resources like GPIO pins, UART buffers, peripheral state, and shared memory. You know exactly when a piece

43

of data can be read or written. You know that two parts of your program can't use the same resource in conflicting ways. And the compiler becomes your strongest ally in maintaining correctness across every line of firmware you write.

This discipline not only helps you avoid bugs—it also enables you to write reusable, composable drivers and system components that scale cleanly across projects. As you move into more advanced embedded topics like concurrency, timers, and communication protocols, this foundation of ownership and borrowing will continue to guide the structure and safety of your code.

Writing Idiomatic, Minimal Rust Code for Microcontrollers

Writing idiomatic Rust means expressing your ideas in a way that is natural to the language—leveraging its strengths while following patterns that are well-understood, efficient, and safe. When you bring that mindset into embedded development, you're working with a special set of constraints: no operating system, limited memory, no dynamic allocation, and a focus on determinism. But Rust gives you a powerful foundation to write clean, minimal, and expressive code—even in bare-metal microcontroller environments.

To write idiomatic embedded Rust, you start by embracing the things that make Rust unique: ownership, strong typing, zero-cost abstractions, and exhaustive compile-time checks. At the same time, you must respect the embedded environment—where minimalism isn't just an aesthetic choice, but a practical requirement.

Use #![no_std] and Limit Your Dependencies

An embedded application should explicitly opt out of the standard library. You begin each program with:

```
#![no_std]
```

```
#![no_main]
```

This tells the compiler that your firmware does not rely on standard OS features and will use `core` as its base library. From this point forward, everything you write should avoid dynamic allocation, file I/O, threads, or

44

heap-backed containers like `Vec`. You'll lean on fixed-size arrays, static memory, and stack-only allocations.

Minimalism also applies to external dependencies. Avoid pulling in crates you don't fully understand or that do more than you need. Keep your `Cargo.toml` lean. Every crate adds compile time, binary size, and potential risks. Focus on just what's required: your HAL, `cortex-m`, `cortex-m-rt`, a panic handler, and maybe `heapless` for fixed-capacity containers.

Structure Initialization Cleanly

Most embedded systems begin by configuring clocks, splitting GPIO ports, and preparing peripherals. Your `#[entry]` function should do this step-by-step, using safe abstractions and giving each resource a clear owner.

Here's a clean and idiomatic start-up sequence using the STM32F3 HAL:

```rust
#![no_std]
#![no_main]

use cortex_m_rt::entry;
use panic_halt as _;
use stm32f3xx_hal::{pac, prelude::*};

#[entry]
fn main() -> ! {
    let dp = pac::Peripherals::take().unwrap();

    let mut rcc = dp.RCC.constrain();
    let mut gpioe = dp.GPIOE.split(&mut rcc.ahb);

    let mut led =
gpioe.pe9.into_push_pull_output(&mut gpioe.moder,
&mut gpioe.otyper);

    loop {
        led.toggle().ok();
        cortex_m::asm::delay(8_000_000);
    }
}
```

This program toggles an LED connected to pin PE9. Each peripheral is initialized in a clean sequence. The GPIO pin becomes a distinct object, and its type encodes its mode (Output<PushPull>), preventing you from accidentally misusing it later.

Use the Type System to Enforce Correctness

Rust encourages you to use the type system to express invariants. In embedded Rust, this helps you model hardware configuration stages in code, making invalid states impossible to represent.

For example, consider a peripheral like a UART interface. It shouldn't be used until it's properly configured. You can represent that in Rust using different types:

```rust
struct UartUninitialized;
struct UartConfigured;

impl UartUninitialized {
    fn configure(self, baud: u32) -> UartConfigured
{
        // Setup code here
        UartConfigured { /* ... */ }
    }
}

impl UartConfigured {
    fn send(&self, byte: u8) {
        // Actual transmit logic
    }
}
```

Now your code won't compile unless the UART is configured first. This is the type-state pattern, and it's a powerful way to guide users of your API toward safe behavior—something C cannot enforce.

Pass Data by Reference or Ownership, Never With Globals

Avoid using global mutable variables unless there's a very strong reason—and even then, access them using synchronization primitives or safe wrappers like cortex_m::singleton!. Prefer passing references to functions so lifetimes and borrow rules are enforced.

46

Here's an idiomatic function that writes to a serial interface:

```
fn write_message<T:
embedded_hal::serial::Write<u8>>(serial: &mut T) {
    for byte in b"Hello!\r\n" {
        nb::block!(serial.write(*byte)).ok();
    }
}
```

This function is generic, safe, and minimal. It takes a mutable reference to any type that implements the `Write<u8>` trait. You get flexibility, reusability, and correctness—all without dynamic dispatch.

Model Peripherals as Owned, Independent Objects

When using HALs, peripherals are typically split into independently owned objects. This helps you avoid unsafe shared access and encourages modular design.

Once you split a GPIO port, each pin becomes an independent object. Treat them that way. Avoid passing around raw register pointers or trying to manually reconfigure hardware after it's been initialized. Trust the HAL to handle it safely and efficiently.

If you need to reuse hardware from multiple locations—say a buffer used by both a timer and the main loop—wrap it in a synchronization primitive, or move toward RTIC or Embassy for structured task concurrency.

Minimize Work in Interrupt Handlers

Rust gives you the safety to write interrupt code, but you should still minimize what happens inside those handlers. Let interrupts set flags, push data to a ring buffer, or update a shared atomic variable. Let your main loop do the heavy lifting.

Here's a pattern using `heapless::spsc::Queue` in a `static` context:

```
use heapless::spsc::Queue;
use cortex_m::interrupt::{free, Mutex};
use core::cell::RefCell;
```

```
static QUEUE: Mutex<RefCell<Option<Queue<u8, 8>>>>
= Mutex::new(RefCell::new(None));

#[entry]
fn main() -> ! {
    let q = Queue::new();
    free(|cs| {
        QUEUE.borrow(cs).replace(Some(q));
    });

    loop {
        // Pop from queue, process messages
    }
}
```

The queue is safely shared between the main loop and an interrupt handler. Rust's ownership model, `Mutex`, and `RefCell` ensure that this sharing is safe and explicit.

Avoid Unsafe Unless Absolutely Necessary

Sometimes, you'll encounter hardware access patterns that require `unsafe`. This might happen when accessing `static mut`, or writing to a volatile memory region directly. When you do use `unsafe`, isolate it. Contain it inside a function. Wrap it in a safe API. Comment it thoroughly.

For example, this might be used to write to a specific address:

```
unsafe fn write_reg(addr: u32, value: u32) {
    core::ptr::write_volatile(addr as *mut u32,
value);
}
```

Wrap that in a safe abstraction if possible. The goal is to minimize `unsafe` blocks and make their correctness easy to verify.

Use Crate Features Strategically

Many HALs and BSPs use Cargo features to conditionally include support for specific chips or modules. Enable only the features you need:

```
[dependencies.stm32f3xx-hal]
```

```
version = "0.9"

features = ["stm32f303", "rt"]
```

Keeping features minimal reduces your binary size and speeds up build times. It also avoids unused code paths that might contain bugs or misconfigurations.

Writing idiomatic and minimal Rust for microcontrollers is not about doing less—it's about doing more with certainty. Rust enables you to write firmware that is clear, composable, and safe by design. You eliminate undefined behavior not by chance, but by construction. Every resource is accounted for. Every access is correct or caught at compile time. And every peripheral is used in a way that matches its real-world behavior.

As your projects grow, the structure you build now will pay off in maintainability, testability, and confidence. You'll spend less time hunting for subtle bugs and more time building reliable systems that just work—on hardware that demands nothing less.

Chapter 4: GPIO, LEDs, and Device Crates

Interacting with physical hardware is where embedded development becomes real. You're no longer just compiling code and watching logs—you're controlling real pins, blinking real LEDs, and reading real signals. This chapter is where we begin to bridge the software you write with the hardware it runs on. We'll focus on how to control general-purpose input/output (GPIO) pins, how to use board support crates (BSPs), how `embedded-hal` traits help standardize hardware interaction, and how to structure your code so it's safe, reusable, and adaptable across devices.

Using Board Support Crates (BSPs)

When you're writing embedded Rust applications, you're not just programming a chip—you're programming a specific board with its own wiring, pin mappings, clock configuration, and possibly extra components like LEDs, sensors, or USB connectors. And while the underlying microcontroller might be powerful, it won't do anything meaningful unless it's correctly initialized. This is where Board Support Crates—commonly referred to as **BSPs**—become essential.

A **Board Support Crate** is a Rust crate that encapsulates all the boilerplate and configuration details specific to a particular development board. It typically builds on top of a **Hardware Abstraction Layer (HAL)** for the microcontroller family used on that board. The BSP gives you a set of well-defined entry points and sensible defaults for clocks, I/O pin mapping, peripheral setup, and sometimes even pre-wired device interfaces like LEDs or USB.

Using a BSP removes much of the trial and error from getting a board up and running, especially if you're just getting started or switching between different boards in a project.

Why BSPs Matter in Embedded Rust

Without a BSP, you'd need to manually initialize your microcontroller from scratch. This includes setting up the clock tree, managing resets, mapping

GPIO pins, configuring memory regions, and more. It can be time-consuming and fragile if done by hand—especially when dealing with hardware-specific register mappings.

A BSP solves this by prepackaging all of those tasks using safe and idiomatic Rust code. It also tends to define convenient aliases for the physical pins on the board, which helps prevent wiring mistakes and misconfiguration.

For example, on the Raspberry Pi Pico board, the onboard LED is physically connected to GPIO 25. You could manually write code to enable GPIO 25, configure it as an output, and then toggle its state. But using the rp-pico BSP, you simply use pins.led, and the crate gives you a ready-to-use abstraction over that specific pin.

Installing a BSP in Your Project

To get started with a BSP, you need to add it to your project's Cargo.toml. Let's say you're working with the Raspberry Pi Pico:

```
[dependencies]

rp-pico = "0.8"
```

Behind the scenes, this BSP pulls in the rp2040-hal, which contains the hardware abstractions for the RP2040 chip, and sets up the board-specific configuration for you.

Once added, you can use the crate in your main.rs:

```
use rp_pico::hal as hal;

use hal::pac;

use hal::prelude::*;
```

You now have access to the HAL modules, the PAC (Peripheral Access Crate), and convenient traits for GPIO, clocks, timers, and more.

Using the BSP to Configure Peripherals

The BSP usually provides a `Pins` struct or something similar that lets you access all of the GPIOs mapped and labeled in a way that matches the silkscreen on your board.

Here's an example that initializes the LED on the Raspberry Pi Pico using the `rp-pico` BSP:

```
#![no_std]
#![no_main]

use cortex_m_rt::entry;
use panic_halt as _;
use rp_pico::hal::{self, pac,
clocks::init_clocks_and_plls, sio::Sio,
watchdog::Watchdog, gpio::PushPullOutput};
use hal::prelude::*;

#[entry]
fn main() -> ! {
    let mut peripherals =
pac::Peripherals::take().unwrap();
    let mut watchdog =
Watchdog::new(peripherals.WATCHDOG);

    let clocks = init_clocks_and_plls(
        rp_pico::XOSC_CRYSTAL_FREQ,
        peripherals.XOSC,
        peripherals.CLOCKS,
        peripherals.PLL_SYS,
        peripherals.PLL_USB,
        &mut peripherals.RESETS,
        &mut watchdog,
    )
    .ok()
    .unwrap();

    let sio = Sio::new(peripherals.SIO);

    let pins = rp_pico::Pins::new(
        peripherals.IO_BANK0,
        peripherals.PADS_BANK0,
        sio.gpio_bank0,
```

```
        &mut peripherals.RESETS,
    );

    let mut led_pin =
pins.led.into_push_pull_output();

    loop {
        led_pin.set_high().unwrap();
        cortex_m::asm::delay(12_000_000);
        led_pin.set_low().unwrap();
        cortex_m::asm::delay(12_000_000);
    }
}
```

In this program:

The BSP provides `rp_pico::Pins`, which includes the `led` pin already aliased for you.

You don't need to look up datasheets or manually map GPIO 25. The crate abstracts that detail in a clean and safe way.

The HAL handles clock setup, watchdog initialization, and SIO configuration—all through predictable, well-tested interfaces.

Extending Beyond LEDs

While LEDs are often used as a first test, BSPs usually provide convenient aliases for other devices on the board. For example:

Buttons, pre-wired to GPIOs

Onboard sensors like accelerometers

USB interface setup

UART, I2C, and SPI ports with labeled pins

The goal is to make you productive faster by removing guesswork and providing working defaults. If your board includes an onboard temperature sensor, the BSP may provide a helper method to read from it. If it has a USB port, the BSP may configure USB clocks and pin mappings automatically, freeing you to focus on functionality rather than infrastructure.

53

Real-World BSP Use Case: nRF52840-DK

For Nordic's nRF52840-DK board, the `nrf52840-dk` crate provides similar value. It wraps the `nrf-hal` crate and gives you immediate access to board-specific features like:

LEDs mapped to labeled GPIOs (`led1`, `led2`, etc.)

Buttons with meaningful names (`button1`, `button2`)

Preconfigured SoftDevice support for Bluetooth (if needed)

Using this BSP, you can immediately begin interacting with hardware without studying schematics or writing complex GPIO configuration code.

```
[dependencies]

nrf52840-dk = "0.1"

let p =
nrf52840_hal::pac::Peripherals::take().unwrap();

let port0 = p.P0.split();

let led1 =
board.leds.led1.into_push_pull_output(Level::Low);
```

Everything you need is exposed in an intuitive and idiomatic Rust interface.

BSPs are one of the most powerful productivity tools in the embedded Rust ecosystem. They save time, reduce errors, and let you work at a higher level of abstraction without giving up performance or control. Whether you're blinking an LED or setting up a full USB peripheral stack, using a BSP means your code starts on a solid, reliable foundation.

And because BSPs are built the "Rust way"—with type safety, ownership, and composability in mind—they enable clean APIs, prevent misconfiguration, and help enforce correct usage of your hardware at compile time.

Blinking LEDs with GPIO

Controlling an LED is one of the most fundamental tasks in embedded programming, and for good reason. It's simple, it gives you immediate visual feedback, and it teaches you how to work with GPIO—general-purpose input/output—which is one of the core hardware interfaces in any microcontroller. When you can configure a pin, toggle its state, and see the effect on an LED, you've confirmed that your build environment, board setup, and peripheral control are all functioning properly.

GPIO refers to the microcontroller's ability to control or read digital voltage signals on physical pins. When a pin is configured as an **output**, you can drive it high (typically 3.3V) or low (0V) to power a connected device like an LED. When configured as an **input**, you can read its state and detect things like button presses.

In this example, we'll focus on output. An LED is typically connected in series with a resistor to a GPIO pin and either ground or power. Driving the pin high or low turns the LED on or off depending on the wiring. Most development boards connect an onboard LED to a specific pin—often referred to by a BSP alias like `led` or `led_pin`.

In Rust, you use your board's HAL and BSP to configure the pin safely, then you can use `set_high()` and `set_low()` methods to control its state. These methods come from the `OutputPin` trait defined by the `embedded-hal` crate.

Blinking an LED with the Raspberry Pi Pico

Let's walk through a complete example using the Raspberry Pi Pico and the `rp-pico` crate. The onboard LED is connected to GPIO pin 25, but the BSP provides a convenient alias so we don't need to worry about that directly.

Here is a full, minimal Rust program that blinks the LED:

```
#![no_std]
#![no_main]

use cortex_m_rt::entry;
use panic_halt as _;

use rp_pico::hal::{
    clocks::init_clocks_and_plls,
    gpio::PushPullOutput,
    pac,
    prelude::*,
```

```
    sio::Sio,
    watchdog::Watchdog,
};

#[entry]
fn main() -> ! {
    let mut peripherals =
pac::Peripherals::take().unwrap();
    let core =
pac::CorePeripherals::take().unwrap();

    let mut watchdog =
Watchdog::new(peripherals.WATCHDOG);

    let clocks = init_clocks_and_plls(
        rp_pico::XOSC_CRYSTAL_FREQ,
        peripherals.XOSC,
        peripherals.CLOCKS,
        peripherals.PLL_SYS,
        peripherals.PLL_USB,
        &mut peripherals.RESETS,
        &mut watchdog,
    )
    .ok()
    .unwrap();

    let sio = Sio::new(peripherals.SIO);

    let pins = rp_pico::Pins::new(
        peripherals.IO_BANK0,
        peripherals.PADS_BANK0,
        sio.gpio_bank0,
        &mut peripherals.RESETS,
    );

    let mut led = pins.led.into_push_pull_output();

    loop {
        led.set_high().unwrap();
        cortex_m::asm::delay(12_000_000);

        led.set_low().unwrap();
```

```
        cortex_m::asm::delay(12_000_000);
    }
}
```

Breaking Down the Code

Initialization: The peripherals are taken using `pac::Peripherals::take()`, which ensures safe, singleton access to the chip's hardware blocks. You also configure clocks and enable system peripherals using the HAL-provided functions.

GPIO Configuration: The `pins` object is built using the board's BSP. It gives you named access to all the board's physical pins. The call to `pins.led.into_push_pull_output()` converts the GPIO pin into a digital output mode. The LED pin now implements the `OutputPin` trait.

LED Control Loop: Inside the infinite `loop`, the LED is turned on with `set_high()`, a delay is introduced, and then the LED is turned off with `set_low()`, followed by another delay. This loop runs forever, causing the LED to blink visibly.

Delays: The use of `cortex_m::asm::delay()` introduces a busy-wait loop that consumes CPU cycles. It's not precise for real-time control but works fine for simple visual delays. You could replace this with hardware timers later for more precise behavior.

Handling GPIO Errors

The `set_high()` and `set_low()` methods return a `Result<(), PinError>`. In this example, we use `.unwrap()` to panic on error. This is fine for learning or prototyping, but in production code, you should check for errors explicitly or use `.ok()` if you want to safely ignore them.

```
led.set_high().ok(); // Safe, ignores error
```

Or handle it explicitly:

```
if let Err(e) = led.set_high() {

    // Log the error or handle fallback
```

```
}
```

In most HALs, the GPIO pins rarely fail unless you're reusing them across contexts or the configuration is incorrect. But writing defensively ensures more robust firmware.

Real-World Blink Exercise

Here's a practical exercise you can try to reinforce what you've learned:

Goal: Modify the LED blink rate using a variable delay that increases each loop until it resets.

```
let mut delay = 2_000_000;

loop {
    led.set_high().ok();
    cortex_m::asm::delay(delay);
    led.set_low().ok();
    cortex_m::asm::delay(delay);

    delay += 500_000;
    if delay > 10_000_000 {
        delay = 2_000_000;
    }
}
```

This creates a fading blink pattern—starting fast and gradually slowing down. It demonstrates how you can modify behavior dynamically even without an RTOS or external library.

Blinking an LED may seem trivial, but it's foundational. It's your first tangible interaction with hardware. It confirms that your GPIO configuration is correct, your board is responsive, and your Rust environment is properly set up. More importantly, it introduces a repeatable pattern you'll use constantly—configure a peripheral, interact through a safe interface, and rely on the type system to protect you from misusing hardware.

Once you're comfortable blinking an LED, you're ready to start reading inputs, handling interrupts, working with timers, and communicating with external devices. But no matter how complex your system becomes, the simple act of toggling a GPIO pin remains at the core of embedded development—and Rust makes that both safe and efficient.

Understanding embedded-hal Traits

One of the major strengths of embedded Rust is its ability to separate hardware-specific details from reusable logic. This is made possible by the embedded-hal crate, which defines a common set of **traits**—that is, standardized interfaces—for interacting with embedded hardware. These traits enable portability, testability, and abstraction in a way that traditional C libraries rarely achieve.

The embedded-hal crate is a collection of Rust traits that define how common embedded peripherals should behave. These include digital input/output, analog input, serial communication (UART), SPI, I2C, PWM, timers, and more.

What makes these traits powerful is that they are **hardware-agnostic**. That means you can write a driver that talks to an I2C device, like a temperature sensor, and that driver will work with any microcontroller platform that implements the embedded-hal I2C traits.

You don't need to rewrite or adapt your code when switching from an STM32 board to a Nordic nRF board or a Raspberry Pi Pico. As long as the HAL for your chip implements the embedded-hal traits correctly, your code will just work.

Understanding Traits with GPIO Example

Let's start with a simple trait: digital output.

The OutputPin trait from embedded-hal defines an interface for setting a pin high or low. Here's a simplified version of the trait:

```
pub trait OutputPin {
    type Error;

    fn set_high(&mut self) -> Result<(),
Self::Error>;
    fn set_low(&mut self) -> Result<(),
Self::Error>;
```

```
}
```

If a type implements this trait, you can call `.set_high()` and `.set_low()` to control a pin. Every GPIO pin object in a HAL that supports `embedded-hal` implements this trait, which means you can write generic code like this:

```
use embedded_hal::digital::v2::OutputPin;

fn blink_once<P: OutputPin>(pin: &mut P) {
    pin.set_high().ok();
    delay();
    pin.set_low().ok();
    delay();
}
```

This function works with any output pin on any board, as long as the pin type implements `OutputPin`. You can pass in a pin from STM32, RP2040, or any other HAL. This is **true polymorphism** without dynamic dispatch—everything is resolved at compile time, so there's no performance penalty.

Traits for Input Pins

Digital input is handled by the `InputPin` trait. It defines how to read the logic level on a pin:

```
pub trait InputPin {

    type Error;


    fn is_high(&self) -> Result<bool, Self::Error>;

    fn is_low(&self) -> Result<bool, Self::Error>;

}
```

You can use this trait to check whether a button is pressed or not. For example:

```
fn wait_for_button<P: InputPin>(button: &P) {
    while button.is_low().unwrap() {
        // Wait until button is pressed (goes high)
    }
```

```
}
```

Again, this function is fully generic. You can use it with any input pin, regardless of the board you're on.

Traits for Serial Communication (UART)

Serial communication is handled through two traits: `Read` and `Write`. These are often used for UART/USART peripherals.

```
pub trait Write<Word> {
    type Error;

    fn write(&mut self, word: Word) ->
nb::Result<(), Self::Error>;
    fn flush(&mut self) -> nb::Result<(),
Self::Error>;
}
pub trait Read<Word> {
    type Error;

    fn read(&mut self) -> nb::Result<Word,
Self::Error>;
}
```

The `nb::Result` type means the operation is **non-blocking**. If the peripheral isn't ready, it returns `WouldBlock`. This allows you to build reactive, interrupt-safe code without busy-waiting.

Here's a function that writes a string of bytes over any UART that implements `embedded-hal::serial::Write<u8>`:

```
use embedded_hal::serial::Write;
use nb::block;

fn send_string<S: Write<u8>>(serial: &mut S, data:
&[u8]) {
    for byte in data {
        block!(serial.write(*byte)).unwrap();
    }
    block!(serial.flush()).unwrap();
}
```

This function works regardless of which microcontroller you're on. You don't need to rewrite it just because the hardware changed.

Working Example: Blinking an LED Using Only a Trait

Let's say you have a driver that blinks an LED and you want to write it generically. Here's how you might define it:

```
use embedded_hal::digital::v2::OutputPin;

pub struct Led<P>
where
    P: OutputPin,
{
    pin: P,
}

impl<P> Led<P>
where
    P: OutputPin,
{
    pub fn new(pin: P) -> Self {
        Self { pin }
    }

    pub fn blink(&mut self, delay_cycles: u32) {
        self.pin.set_high().ok();
        cortex_m::asm::delay(delay_cycles);
        self.pin.set_low().ok();
        cortex_m::asm::delay(delay_cycles);
    }
}
```

In your main application, you can create an `Led` object from any output-capable pin and blink it:

```
let mut led =
Led::new(pins.led.into_push_pull_output());
loop {
    led.blink(8_000_000);
}
```

This is idiomatic embedded Rust. It abstracts behavior into reusable components while remaining tightly coupled to hardware performance.

Writing Your Own Trait-Based Driver

Let's say you want to write a driver for an I2C temperature sensor. You don't care which I2C peripheral is used—you just want something that implements the I2C trait.

Here's a simplified driver for a sensor with address `0x48` and a command to read the temperature:

```
use embedded_hal::blocking::i2c::WriteRead;

pub struct TempSensor<I2C> {
    i2c: I2C,
    address: u8,
}

impl<I2C, E> TempSensor<I2C>
where
    I2C: WriteRead<Error = E>,
{
    pub fn new(i2c: I2C, address: u8) -> Self {
        Self { i2c, address }
    }

    pub fn read_temperature(&mut self) ->
Result<u16, E> {
        let mut buffer = [0; 2];
        self.i2c.write_read(self.address, &[0x00],
&mut buffer)?;
        Ok(u16::from_be_bytes(buffer))
    }
}
```

This driver works on any microcontroller as long as the I2C implementation follows the `WriteRead` trait. That's the power of `embedded-hal`: decoupling logic from hardware.

The `embedded-hal` traits are the backbone of portable, maintainable embedded Rust. They allow you to write drivers and logic once and reuse them

63

across projects and platforms. Whether you're toggling GPIO pins, reading sensor data, or communicating over SPI or I2C, `embedded-hal` gives you a clean, predictable interface that works everywhere.

By building your firmware on top of these traits, you're setting yourself up for long-term flexibility. Your code will scale across microcontrollers, integrate easily with new drivers, and remain robust—even as the hardware around it evolves. This is not just good embedded Rust—it's good embedded engineering.

Abstracting Hardware Access

In embedded systems programming, one of your primary responsibilities is to communicate directly with hardware—controlling peripherals, managing GPIO pins, reading sensor values, and so on. This often involves interacting with hardware registers and tightly coupled memory-mapped interfaces, which in traditional systems programming languages like C is typically done through unsafe pointer manipulation. While this gives you full control, it also exposes you to serious risks: undefined behavior, data races, and accidental corruption of critical memory.

Rust approaches this challenge differently. It allows you to build safe, predictable, zero-cost abstractions over low-level hardware, making it possible to write embedded firmware that is both expressive and secure. The idea is to **encapsulate hardware behavior behind strongly typed, safe APIs** that enforce correct usage patterns at compile time—so you don't just hope your code is right, you know the compiler is checking it for you.

Let's begin with a basic but common peripheral: an LED connected to a GPIO pin. Your HAL gives you low-level access to the pin and lets you call `.set_high()` or `.set_low()` on it. That's already useful. But what if you wanted to abstract this behavior into a reusable component?

Instead of scattering pin operations across your codebase, you can create a simple `Led` wrapper. This approach improves readability and testability, and makes it easier to swap the underlying hardware without affecting the rest of your logic.

Here's a fully safe abstraction around a digital output pin:

```rust
use embedded_hal::digital::v2::OutputPin;

pub struct Led<P>
where
    P: OutputPin,
{
    pin: P,
}

impl<P> Led<P>
where
    P: OutputPin,
{
    pub fn new(pin: P) -> Self {
        Self { pin }
    }

    pub fn on(&mut self) {
        let _ = self.pin.set_high();
    }

    pub fn off(&mut self) {
        let _ = self.pin.set_low();
    }

    pub fn toggle(&mut self) {
        // This is only available if the HAL also
implements ToggleableOutputPin
        // We'll simulate it here using manual
logic:
        // You would extend this with is_set_high()
if your pin supports InputPin too.
    }
}
```

In this example, the Led type is generic over any type that implements the OutputPin trait. That means it will work with GPIO pins from any supported platform. You can now write led.on() and led.off() anywhere in your firmware, and you don't have to repeat pin-level logic throughout your application.

Enforcing Correct State with Type-State Pattern

Some peripherals—like UART, SPI, or I2C—require a specific configuration before they can be used. In traditional firmware development, it's easy to forget a step or call a function in the wrong order. Rust gives you a pattern known as **type states**, which allows you to encode the state of a peripheral directly in the type system. This prevents invalid states and illegal transitions from even compiling.

Here's a simple type-state pattern for an uninitialized and initialized peripheral:

```
struct UartUninit;
struct UartReady;

pub struct Uart<State> {
    config: u32,
    state: core::marker::PhantomData<State>,
}

impl Uart<UartUninit> {
    pub fn configure(self, baudrate: u32) ->
Uart<UartReady> {
        // Apply configuration
        Uart {
            config: baudrate,
            state: core::marker::PhantomData,
        }
    }
}

impl Uart<UartReady> {
    pub fn send(&self, byte: u8) {
        // Write byte to TX register
    }
}
```

With this setup:

You **can't call send()** unless the UART is properly configured.

If you try to use Uart<UartUninit> in the wrong place, the compiler will raise a type mismatch error.

This prevents entire categories of runtime bugs that would otherwise require hours of debugging or could cause critical failures in production.

Hiding Unsafe Behind Safe APIs

There are situations where unsafe code is necessary—especially when dealing with raw hardware registers, memory-mapped I/O, or static mutables. The idiomatic Rust approach is to **confine all unsafe code inside safe, well-tested abstractions** and expose only safe interfaces to the rest of your code.

Here's an example where you use an unsafe block internally but keep the public API completely safe:

```rust
pub struct Register {
    address: *mut u32,
}

impl Register {
    pub fn new(address: usize) -> Self {
        Self {
            address: address as *mut u32,
        }
    }

    pub fn read(&self) -> u32 {
        unsafe {
core::ptr::read_volatile(self.address) }
    }

    pub fn write(&self, value: u32) {
        unsafe {
core::ptr::write_volatile(self.address, value) }
    }
}
```

Anyone using this `Register` API cannot misuse it—they only have access to `read()` and `write()` methods, which enforce correct access patterns and minimize the risks associated with volatile memory operations.

This practice is particularly important in HAL development. A well-designed HAL crate exposes a safe API that wraps all low-level, unsafe operations behind internally verified code paths.

Designing a Safe Driver Interface

Let's go further and write a driver abstraction for an LED matrix. You want to expose an API like set_pixel(x, y) or clear_display()—and you want to support different hardware platforms.

Here's a basic setup using embedded-hal traits for SPI communication:

```
use embedded_hal::blocking::spi::Write;

pub struct LedMatrix<SPI> {
    spi: SPI,
}

impl<SPI, E> LedMatrix<SPI>
where
    SPI: Write<u8, Error = E>,
{
    pub fn new(spi: SPI) -> Self {
        Self { spi }
    }

    pub fn draw_frame(&mut self, frame: &[u8]) ->
Result<(), E> {
        self.spi.write(frame)
    }

    pub fn clear(&mut self) -> Result<(), E> {
        self.spi.write(&[0x00; 64])
    }
}
```

This driver:

Works with any SPI implementation that satisfies the embedded-hal trait.

Avoids unsafe code completely.

Is portable across boards and microcontroller families.

This is how you should build every hardware interface in your firmware—by layering safe abstractions over the embedded-hal traits and hiding platform-specific details in the HAL or BSP.

68

Real-World Exercise: Safe LED Wrapper

Create a type-safe LED struct that only accepts a pin already configured as an output:

```
use embedded_hal::digital::v2::OutputPin;

pub struct SafeLed<P: OutputPin> {
    pin: P,
}

impl<P: OutputPin> SafeLed<P> {
    pub fn new(pin: P) -> Self {
        Self { pin }
    }

    pub fn set(&mut self, on: bool) {
        if on {
            self.pin.set_high().ok();
        } else {
            self.pin.set_low().ok();
        }
    }
}
```

This type ensures at compile time that only output-capable pins can be passed into your `SafeLed` type. Try misusing it with an input pin and the compiler will reject the code immediately.

Safe abstraction is one of Rust's biggest advantages in embedded systems development. Rather than writing raw pointer arithmetic and scattering register access across your firmware, you design structured APIs that reflect real hardware constraints and enforce them with the compiler. Whether you're wrapping a single pin or implementing a full driver stack, this approach gives you predictability, testability, and peace of mind.

The key takeaway is this: **write unsafe code once, safely wrap it, and expose only reliable, high-level interfaces**. This not only reduces bugs but also makes your firmware more reusable, maintainable, and portable across platforms.

Chapter 5: Interrupts, Timers, and Real-Time Behavior

Up to this point, we've written embedded Rust firmware that runs in a simple infinite loop, toggles GPIOs, and interacts with peripherals one step at a time. That works well for straightforward tasks, but real systems need to respond to events asynchronously—such as a timer expiring, a sensor value changing, or a communication packet arriving. You don't want to sit in a busy loop polling everything. Instead, you want **interrupts** and **timers** to drive your system behavior with precision and responsiveness.

This chapter will teach you how to write safe and efficient interrupt handlers, use hardware timers for delay and task scheduling, and introduce real-time execution concepts using the RTIC framework. We'll also walk through how to share resources between main code and interrupts in a way that's safe and race-free.

Writing Safe Interrupt Handlers

Interrupts are one of the most powerful features of a microcontroller. They allow your program to respond immediately to external events—such as a timer expiring, a button being pressed, or data arriving on a communication line—without constantly checking for changes in a loop. But with that power comes risk. Interrupts interrupt your code, potentially at any time, and if you're not careful about how data is accessed and shared, you can end up with subtle, unpredictable bugs.

Rust helps eliminate these risks by enforcing strict memory safety rules—even in interrupt handlers. Writing interrupt-safe code in Rust means structuring your data, your control flow, and your hardware access in ways that are explicit and statically verified. In this section, you'll learn how to register interrupt handlers in embedded Rust, how to safely access shared state from them, and how to structure your firmware to avoid race conditions or undefined behavior.

Declaring and Registering an Interrupt Handler

In a typical embedded C project, you'd define a function with a special name and the toolchain would wire it into the interrupt vector table. Rust does this more explicitly using the #[interrupt] attribute from the cortex-m-rt crate, which maps your handler to a specific hardware interrupt vector based on your microcontroller's Peripheral Access Crate (PAC).

For example, if you're using a timer interrupt called TIM2, your handler looks like this:

```
#[interrupt]

fn TIM2() {

    // Handle the interrupt

}
```

When you build your firmware, the #[interrupt] attribute ensures that this function is linked into the vector table under the correct index. If you mistype the interrupt name or if your PAC doesn't include that interrupt, you'll get a compile-time error—which is exactly what you want.

However, just writing the handler is not enough. For most peripherals, you must also **enable the interrupt** in both the peripheral configuration and the NVIC (Nested Vector Interrupt Controller). You do that like this:

```
use cortex_m::peripheral::NVIC;


let mut nvic = unsafe {
cortex_m::peripheral::NVIC::steal() };

unsafe {
NVIC::unmask(stm32f3xx_hal::pac::Interrupt::TIM2)
};
```

You must also configure the peripheral (in this case, a timer) to raise the interrupt at the appropriate time, such as when a counter overflows or an event flag is set.

The Challenge of Shared State

The real challenge in writing interrupt handlers is not registering them—it's managing shared state safely. An interrupt can occur at almost any point in your program, so if it tries to read or modify a variable that your main application is also accessing, you have a **data race**. Rust does not allow data races, even in bare-metal code. If you try to share mutable data between `main()` and an interrupt without precautions, your code won't compile.

To solve this, Rust gives you several options:

Use `Mutex<RefCell<T>>` with critical sections.

Use `core::sync::atomic` types.

Use frameworks like RTIC to manage task-level isolation automatically.

We'll start with the standard `cortex_m::interrupt::Mutex`.

Safe Shared Access Using Mutex

Rust's `cortex_m` crate provides an interrupt-safe `Mutex`, which lets you temporarily disable interrupts while accessing shared data. Here's a basic pattern:

```
use cortex_m::interrupt::{self, Mutex};

use core::cell::RefCell;



static LED_STATE: Mutex<RefCell<Option<bool>>> =
Mutex::new(RefCell::new(None));
```

Inside `main()`, you initialize the shared variable:

```
#[entry]
fn main() -> ! {
    interrupt::free(|cs| {
        LED_STATE.borrow(cs).replace(Some(false));
    });

    loop {
        // Application logic
    }
```

```
}                                             |
```

And in your interrupt handler:

```
#[interrupt]
fn TIM2() {
    interrupt::free(|cs| {
        if let Some(state) =
LED_STATE.borrow(cs).borrow_mut().as_mut() {
            *state = !*state;
        }
    });
}
```

This works because the `free()` function disables interrupts globally while executing the closure, ensuring that access to `LED_STATE` is mutually exclusive. It's important to keep the critical section short and fast—just update the shared state and exit. Any heavy processing should happen outside the critical section.

This pattern is safe and scalable, but verbose. For small flags or counters, there's a more efficient option.

Using Atomic Types

The `core::sync::atomic` module provides primitives for lock-free shared access to integers and booleans. These are ideal when you want to count events, flip a flag, or synchronize two execution contexts.

Here's a basic example using an atomic counter:

```
use core::sync::atomic::{AtomicU32, Ordering};

static TICK_COUNT: AtomicU32 = AtomicU32::new(0);
```

Increment it in the interrupt:

```
#[interrupt]
fn TIM2() {
    TICK_COUNT.fetch_add(1, Ordering::Relaxed);
}
```

Read it in `main()`:

```
fn main() -> ! {
    loop {
        let ticks =
TICK_COUNT.load(Ordering::Relaxed);
        // Use ticks
    }
}
```

Atomic types are fast and do not require disabling interrupts. They're ideal for simple data exchange between `main()` and an ISR, especially if the data fits in a primitive type.

Dealing with Peripheral State in Interrupts

Many embedded tasks require you to use a hardware peripheral (like a UART or SPI controller) both in your main logic and in an interrupt handler. Accessing peripherals safely is trickier because they're often not `Sync` or `Send`, and their register blocks are unique resources.

One common pattern is to store peripherals in a static `Mutex<RefCell<>>`, like this:

```
use stm32f3xx_hal::pac::USART1;
use core::cell::RefCell;

static UART: Mutex<RefCell<Option<USART1>>> =
Mutex::new(RefCell::new(None));
```

Then move the peripheral into the mutex in `main()`:

```
interrupt::free(|cs| {

UART.borrow(cs).replace(Some(peripherals.USART1));
});
```
And access it safely in the handler:
```
#[interrupt]
fn USART1_EXTI25() {
    interrupt::free(|cs| {
        if let Some(uart) =
UART.borrow(cs).borrow_mut().as_mut() {
            // Read or write UART
        }
    });
```

}

You should always minimize the work done inside the handler. Just grab the data, set a flag, or enqueue a byte into a buffer—and let your main loop handle the rest.

Testing and Debugging Interrupts

Interrupt-driven code can be harder to debug, especially when things happen asynchronously. Some good practices include:

Using LEDs or serial logging to confirm interrupt execution.

Keeping handler logic minimal to isolate timing issues.

Disabling interrupts one-by-one to trace misbehavior.

Using a debugger (e.g., with `probe-rs` and `gdb`) to inspect registers and break on interrupt entry.

Also, when testing, it's helpful to use `cortex-m::peripheral::NVIC::unpend()` to clear a stuck interrupt if your peripheral logic fails to acknowledge it correctly.

Interrupts are fundamental to building responsive and efficient embedded systems. In Rust, they aren't an afterthought—you declare them clearly, configure them precisely, and manage shared access safely. Whether you're toggling an LED, updating a timer counter, or reacting to a UART byte, Rust gives you the tools to structure your interrupt handlers in a way that's safe, testable, and deterministic.

By using `Mutex`, atomic types, and minimal handler design, you avoid common pitfalls like race conditions and memory corruption. And once your needs grow, frameworks like RTIC can take over the heavy lifting of scheduling and synchronization.

Using Timers for Delay and Scheduling

Timers are foundational to embedded development. Whether you're blinking an LED at regular intervals, scheduling sensor reads every second, generating PWM signals, or implementing precise communication timeouts, timers give you a way to measure and control time without burning CPU cycles in busy loops. Rust, through its embedded HALs and microcontroller-specific crates, offers powerful and safe ways to configure and use timers for both blocking delays and non-blocking task scheduling.

How Hardware Timers Work

Most microcontrollers include multiple hardware timers. A timer is essentially a counter that increments at a configured frequency. When the counter reaches a predefined value (known as a *compare match*), or overflows, it can trigger an **event**. This event might:

Set a flag

Raise an interrupt

Toggle a pin

Reset the counter

Timers are incredibly versatile and configurable. You can:

Configure them to run at a specific frequency or for a specific duration

Use them for blocking delays

Use them as one-shot timers or periodic tickers

Trigger interrupts on overflow or match events

How you use a timer depends on your use case, but the basic idea remains: set up the timer peripheral, tell it what kind of timing behavior you want, and act on its output.

Blocking Delays with SysTick or General-Purpose Timers

Let's begin with the simplest use case—creating a blocking delay.

Many HALs provide a `Delay` abstraction that uses either the SysTick timer (a timer built into the Cortex-M core) or a general-purpose timer to block execution for a number of milliseconds or microseconds.

Here's a working example using `stm32f3xx-hal`:

```
use stm32f3xx_hal::{delay::Delay, prelude::*, pac};
```

```rust
#[entry]
fn main() -> ! {
    let dp = pac::Peripherals::take().unwrap();
    let cp = pac::CorePeripherals::take().unwrap();

    let mut flash = dp.FLASH.constrain();
    let mut rcc = dp.RCC.constrain();
    let clocks =
rcc.cfgr.sysclk(8.mhz()).freeze(&mut flash.acr);

    let mut delay = Delay::new(cp.SYST, clocks);

    loop {
        // Blocking delay
        delay.delay_ms(500u16);
        // Toggle an LED or perform action
    }
}
```

In this example, the `delay.delay_ms()` function blocks execution for the specified duration. It's easy to use and ideal for simple use cases like blinking LEDs, soft resets, or startup initialization.

But blocking delays tie up the CPU. If you need to do other work while waiting, you'll need a non-blocking alternative.

Non-Blocking Timers with Interrupts

To run code on a schedule without halting the rest of your system, you configure a timer to raise an **interrupt** when it expires. In the interrupt handler, you perform the time-sensitive task, like updating a counter, toggling a pin, or signaling the main loop.

Here's an example using Timer2 (TIM2) in the `stm32f3xx-hal` to trigger an interrupt every second:

```rust
use stm32f3xx_hal::{pac, prelude::*, timer::{Timer,
Event}};

#[entry]
fn main() -> ! {
    let dp = pac::Peripherals::take().unwrap();
```

```
    let mut flash = dp.FLASH.constrain();
    let mut rcc = dp.RCC.constrain();
    let clocks =
rcc.cfgr.sysclk(8.mhz()).freeze(&mut flash.acr);

    let mut timer = Timer::tim2(dp.TIM2, 1.hz(),
clocks, &mut rcc.apb1);
    timer.listen(Event::Update);

    unsafe {

cortex_m::peripheral::NVIC::unmask(pac::Interrupt::
TIM2);
    }

    loop {
        // Main loop runs uninterrupted
    }
}

#[interrupt]
fn TIM2() {
    // Acknowledge the timer interrupt (must clear
flag)
    let tim2 = unsafe { &*pac::TIM2::ptr() };
    tim2.sr.modify(|_, w| w.uif().clear_bit());

    // Task to execute every second
}
```

This setup runs a task every second in the TIM2 interrupt handler. The key line is timer.listen(Event::Update), which enables the "update event" that fires when the timer overflows. The handler must clear the interrupt flag (uif) to avoid retriggering immediately.

Using non-blocking timers this way is ideal for periodic scheduling, and allows your main() loop (or other system components) to continue running independently.

Practical Use Case: Scheduling a Task at Fixed Intervals

Let's say you want to sample a temperature sensor every 250 milliseconds and log the value. Instead of putting a delay in your main loop, you can use a timer interrupt and set a flag or push data into a queue.

```rust
use core::sync::atomic::{AtomicBool, Ordering};

static READY_TO_SAMPLE: AtomicBool =
AtomicBool::new(false);

#[interrupt]
fn TIM3() {
    // Clear interrupt
    unsafe { (*pac::TIM3::ptr()).sr.modify(|_, w|
w.uif().clear_bit()) };

    READY_TO_SAMPLE.store(true, Ordering::Release);
}

#[entry]
fn main() -> ! {
    setup_timer();

    loop {
        if READY_TO_SAMPLE.swap(false,
Ordering::Acquire) {
            let temp = read_temperature();
            log_value(temp);
        }
    }
}
```

Here, the interrupt sets a flag using an atomic boolean, and the main loop checks and resets the flag. This keeps your sampling logic out of the interrupt and keeps the ISR fast and deterministic.

Using Timers for One-Shot Scheduling

You can also use timers as **one-shot** triggers—meaning the timer fires once after a set delay, then stops. This is useful for deferred actions, soft timeouts, or startup delays.

In most HALs, this just means configuring a timer and not enabling continuous mode:

```
let mut timer = Timer::tim2(dp.TIM2, 1.secs(),
clocks, &mut rcc.apb1);
timer.listen(Event::Update);

// In the interrupt, disable the timer
#[interrupt]
fn TIM2() {
    let tim2 = unsafe { &*pac::TIM2::ptr() };
    tim2.cr1.modify(|_, w| w.cen().clear_bit()); //
Disable timer
    tim2.sr.modify(|_, w| w.uif().clear_bit());  //
Clear interrupt

    // Perform one-time action
}
```

This pattern is also useful for retry logic or scheduling a "wake-up" event after a power-saving sleep.

Higher-Level Scheduling with RTIC

If you're using RTIC (Real-Time Interrupt-driven Concurrency), you don't need to manage timer flags or interrupt handlers manually. Instead, you declare periodic or delayed tasks in your application module and let the framework handle the rest.

Here's how you schedule a periodic task every 200 milliseconds in RTIC:

```
#[rtic::app(device = stm32f3xx_hal::pac)]
mod app {
    #[shared]
    struct Shared {}

    #[local]
    struct Local {}

    #[init]
    fn init(ctx: init::Context) -> (Shared, Local,
init::Monotonics) {
        blink::spawn().ok();
```

```
        (Shared {}, Local {}, init::Monotonics())
    }

    #[task]
    fn blink(ctx: blink::Context) {
        toggle_led();

        blink::spawn_after(200.millis()).ok(); //
Re-schedule
    }
}
```

RTIC handles:

Timekeeping

Task dispatch

Race-free access to shared data

This is one of the cleanest ways to schedule periodic tasks and avoid complexity around timer setup.

Timers are indispensable tools in your embedded Rust toolbox. Whether you're:

Using a blocking delay during initialization

Triggering periodic interrupts for scheduled tasks

Implementing deferred logic or timeouts

Managing precise scheduling through RTIC

…you can count on hardware timers to do the work efficiently and predictably.

Rust's strong type system and ecosystem of HALs ensure that even low-level timer usage can be done safely and clearly. By learning to structure your time-based logic around non-blocking, interrupt-driven patterns, you gain both responsiveness and maintainability—without giving up the reliability and determinism embedded systems demand.

Introduction to Real-Time Execution with RTIC

Writing real-time embedded applications usually involves juggling multiple interrupt sources, managing shared data across contexts, and ensuring that high-priority tasks are not delayed by lower-priority ones. In traditional embedded development, especially in C, you often rely on manual interrupt registration, global flags, volatile variables, and hand-rolled scheduling logic. This approach can work—but it can also lead to unmaintainable code, timing bugs, and race conditions that are hard to spot until something breaks in production.

Rust gives you a much better alternative: **RTIC**—*Real-Time Interrupt-driven Concurrency*. RTIC is a concurrency framework specifically designed for embedded Rust on ARM Cortex-M microcontrollers. It allows you to build time-sensitive and event-driven systems with clear structure, predictable timing, and no need for a traditional RTOS. Instead of relying on a runtime kernel, RTIC compiles everything into static scheduling logic that is determined at build time. The result is small, fast, and safe embedded applications.

RTIC provides a way to define tasks that are triggered by hardware interrupts, software events, or timers. You can assign priorities to these tasks, and RTIC takes care of ensuring that:

Higher-priority tasks can preempt lower-priority ones

Shared resources are accessed safely without manual locks

Task scheduling is deterministic and efficient

Memory is statically allocated (no heap required)

The RTIC model is tightly aligned with how Cortex-M microcontrollers work. Rather than introducing a scheduler loop or a background thread, RTIC uses the existing interrupt system as the primary mechanism for concurrency. Your application becomes a collection of interrupt handlers (tasks), each with its own role and timing constraints, coordinated by the compiler.

This model gives you **real-time responsiveness** without sacrificing **memory safety**, **zero-cost abstraction**, or **modularity**.

Basic Structure of an RTIC Application

An RTIC application is written inside a single module annotated with #[rtic::app]. You specify the device PAC (Peripheral Access Crate) for your target microcontroller, and then define four kinds of components:

#[init] — your program's startup logic (runs once, like main())

#[idle] — optional background loop

#[task] — tasks triggered by interrupts or software

#[monotonic] — optional hardware timers for time-based scheduling

Here's a basic RTIC program that toggles an LED every 500 milliseconds:

```
#[rtic::app(device = stm32f3xx_hal::pac,
peripherals = true)]
mod app {
    use super::*;
    use stm32f3xx_hal::{gpio::gpioe::PE9,
prelude::*, pac, timer::Timer};
    use cortex_m::asm;

    #[shared]
    struct Shared {}

    #[local]
    struct Local {
        led:
PE9<stm32f3xx_hal::gpio::Output<stm32f3xx_hal::gpio
::PushPull>>,
        timer: Timer<pac::TIM2>,
    }

    #[init]
    fn init(ctx: init::Context) -> (Shared, Local,
init::Monotonics) {
        let dp = ctx.device;
        let mut rcc = dp.RCC.constrain();
```

```
        let mut flash = dp.FLASH.constrain();

        let clocks = rcc.cfgr.freeze(&mut
flash.acr);
        let mut gpioe = dp.GPIOE.split(&mut
rcc.ahb);
        let mut led = gpioe
            .pe9
            .into_push_pull_output(&mut
gpioe.moder, &mut gpioe.otyper);

        let mut timer = Timer::tim2(dp.TIM2,
2.hz(), clocks, &mut rcc.apb1);

timer.listen(stm32f3xx_hal::timer::Event::Update);

        (Shared {}, Local { led, timer },
init::Monotonics())
    }

    #[task(binds = TIM2, local = [led, timer])]
    fn toggle_led(ctx: toggle_led::Context) {
        ctx.local.led.toggle().ok();

ctx.local.timer.clear_update_interrupt_flag();
    }
}
```

This code does the following:

Initializes peripherals and configures the system clock

Sets up a general-purpose timer to fire an interrupt twice per second

Handles that interrupt in a task (`toggle_led`) that toggles an LED

All of this is **statically verified and memory safe**.

Priorities and Task Preemption

RTIC assigns a priority to each task based on the interrupt vector it's bound to. Tasks with a higher priority (lower number) can **preempt** lower-priority ones. If a lower-priority task is running and a higher-priority task is triggered,

84

it will immediately interrupt and run the higher-priority one. This gives you fine-grained control over task execution and responsiveness.

You don't explicitly assign priorities in numbers. RTIC derives them from the interrupt vectors or assigns priorities to software tasks automatically based on their definition order.

If two tasks share data, RTIC ensures that only the higher-priority task can preempt the lower-priority one during shared resource access. If two tasks have the **same priority**, RTIC enforces exclusive access using **critical sections** (just like a `Mutex`).

This makes resource sharing safe by construction.

Sharing Data Between Tasks

When you need to share data across tasks, you declare it under the `#[shared]` section of your app. RTIC gives you safe access to shared data using `ctx.shared` and an API like `.lock()`:

```
#[shared]
struct Shared {
    counter: u32,
}

#[task(shared = [counter])]
fn increment(ctx: increment::Context) {
    ctx.shared.counter.lock(|c| {
        *c += 1;
    });
}
```

If `increment()` is preempted while it's holding the lock, it's because the other task accessing `counter` has a higher priority and is allowed to do so safely. RTIC guarantees that only one task can access shared data at a time unless it's `Sync`.

This is one of RTIC's biggest strengths—you can share data across tasks without worrying about mutexes, atomics, or manual critical sections.

Periodic Tasks and Scheduling

In RTIC, you can schedule software tasks using `spawn()` or `schedule()` APIs. If you have a hardware monotonic timer configured (like a SysTick or general-purpose timer), you can spawn tasks after a delay or at fixed intervals.

Here's a periodic task example using `spawn_after`:

```
#[task]
fn heartbeat(ctx: heartbeat::Context) {
    blink_led();
    heartbeat::spawn_after(500.millis()).ok();
}
```

This task reschedules itself every 500 milliseconds, effectively becoming a periodic task without needing a hardware timer interrupt.

If you're using a monotonic timer (like from the `dwt-systick-monotonic` crate), you can use `#[monotonic]` and precise timestamps instead.

Practical Exercise: Button-Triggered Task with Debounce

Let's say you have a button connected to a GPIO pin, and you want to toggle an LED when the button is pressed—but debounce it properly. Here's how to model that with RTIC:

```
#[task(binds = EXTI0, shared = [debounce_flag])]
fn on_button_press(ctx: on_button_press::Context) {
    if !ctx.shared.debounce_flag.get() {
        ctx.shared.debounce_flag.set(true);
        toggle_led::spawn().ok();
        clear_exti_flag();

debounce_clear::spawn_after(30.millis()).ok(); //
Start debounce timer
    }
}

#[task(shared = [debounce_flag])]
fn debounce_clear(ctx: debounce_clear::Context) {
    ctx.shared.debounce_flag.set(false);
}
```

You separate the edge detection (ISR) from the debounce logic. RTIC takes care of the timing and the synchronization between tasks.

RTIC gives you everything you need to build efficient, responsive, and structured embedded applications—without writing a single line of unsafe code. You declare your tasks and their timing behavior, and the compiler takes care of everything else:

Scheduling based on hardware interrupt priorities

Automatic synchronization of shared data

Predictable preemption and real-time responsiveness

No runtime kernel, no heap, and no surprises

By using RTIC, you get the low-level power of bare-metal programming with the safety and composability of modern Rust. Whether you're toggling LEDs, sampling sensors, handling serial input, or coordinating multiple peripherals, RTIC helps you build systems that are maintainable, testable, and safe from race conditions and timing bugs.

Synchronization and Safe Shared Resources

When building embedded systems, especially those that respond to hardware events asynchronously through interrupts or scheduled tasks, you're inevitably going to run into situations where data is accessed by multiple contexts. For instance, a timer interrupt might increment a counter, while the main loop checks that same counter to make decisions. Or you might have a buffer that's filled in one place and consumed in another. This is where synchronization becomes critical.

In unsafe systems programming, shared memory access is one of the biggest sources of bugs—race conditions, data corruption, missed events, and unexpected behavior. Rust tackles these problems head-on with ownership rules, lifetimes, and its strong type system. But when it comes to concurrency in embedded systems, especially without an OS, you still need to be explicit about how you coordinate access to shared state.

Let's say you have a simple shared variable: a counter that tracks how many times an interrupt has fired. In C, you'd make it `volatile` and hope that the compiler behaves correctly. In Rust, that kind of undefined behavior simply isn't allowed.

Here's what the problem looks like:

```rust
static mut COUNTER: u32 = 0;

#[entry]
fn main() -> ! {
    loop {
        unsafe {
            if COUNTER > 100 {
                do_something();
            }
        }
    }
}

#[interrupt]
fn TIM2() {
    unsafe {
        COUNTER += 1;
    }
}
```

This might compile, but it's fundamentally unsafe. There's nothing preventing the main loop and the interrupt from reading or modifying COUNTER at the same time, which leads to undefined behavior. Rust warns you that this is unsafe, and rightly so.

So how do you fix it? You structure your code in a way that makes access exclusive, predictable, and enforced at compile time.

Using Atomic Types for Lock-Free Access

For simple data like booleans, counters, and flags, you should use atomic types from the core::sync::atomic module. These types are safe, fast, and optimized for concurrent access without needing locks or critical sections.

Here's a correct version of the previous example using an atomic counter:

```rust
use core::sync::atomic::{AtomicU32, Ordering};

static COUNTER: AtomicU32 = AtomicU32::new(0);

#[entry]
```

```
fn main() -> ! {
    loop {
        let value =
COUNTER.load(Ordering::Relaxed);
        if value > 100 {
            do_something();
        }
    }
}

#[interrupt]
fn TIM2() {
    COUNTER.fetch_add(1, Ordering::Relaxed);
}
```

This works reliably because the atomic operations ensure that the read and write to COUNTER are indivisible and coherent across contexts. You can choose stricter memory orderings like SeqCst or Acquire/Release if needed, but Relaxed is fine when all you care about is consistent values, not ordering of multiple operations.

Atomic types cover common needs:

AtomicBool for flags

AtomicU8, AtomicU16, AtomicU32, AtomicUsize for counters

compare_exchange for lock-free state machines

If your shared data fits in one of these types, always prefer them over manual locking.

Using Critical Sections for Structured Access

For more complex shared state—such as a struct, a buffer, or a peripheral— you can't use atomic types directly. Instead, you use **critical sections**, which disable interrupts temporarily to give exclusive access to a section of code.

In Rust, this is done with cortex_m::interrupt::free() combined with a Mutex. The Mutex here is not a blocking lock—it's just a safe container that only allows access inside a critical section.

Here's how you do it:

89

```rust
use cortex_m::interrupt::{free, Mutex};
use core::cell::RefCell;

static SHARED: Mutex<RefCell<Option<u32>>> =
Mutex::new(RefCell::new(None));

#[entry]
fn main() -> ! {
    free(|cs| {
        SHARED.borrow(cs).replace(Some(0));
    });

    loop {
        free(|cs| {
            if let Some(count) =
SHARED.borrow(cs).borrow().as_ref() {
                if *count > 10 {
                    do_something();
                }
            }
        });
    }
}

#[interrupt]
fn TIM2() {
    free(|cs| {
        if let Some(count) =
SHARED.borrow(cs).borrow_mut().as_mut() {
            *count += 1;
        }
    });
}
```

This pattern ensures that shared state is never accessed by two contexts at once. The RefCell allows interior mutability, and Mutex enforces that only one context can borrow at a time within a critical section. The cs token passed into the closure enforces scoping and prevents misuse.

You should keep critical sections short and deterministic. Avoid long calculations, blocking operations, or nested critical sections.

Avoiding `static mut` Without Protection

You may be tempted to use `static mut` to store shared variables or peripherals. In most cases, this is unsafe unless wrapped in an abstraction that ensures exclusive access. If you absolutely must use `static mut`, wrap the access inside a `critical_section::with()` or `interrupt::free()` block and mark the access as `unsafe`. But know that there are usually better alternatives.

RTIC, for instance, completely avoids this problem by managing concurrency and data ownership through its task model and `#[shared]` resources. If you're not using RTIC, it's still possible to maintain memory safety—but it takes discipline.

Shared Peripherals Example with Safe Wrapper

Let's say you want to use a UART peripheral in both your main loop and an interrupt. Here's a pattern to do it safely:

```
use cortex_m::interrupt::Mutex;
use core::cell::RefCell;
use stm32f3xx_hal::pac::USART1;

static UART: Mutex<RefCell<Option<USART1>>> =
Mutex::new(RefCell::new(None));

#[entry]
fn main() -> ! {
    let dp = pac::Peripherals::take().unwrap();
    let uart1 = dp.USART1;

    free(|cs| {
        UART.borrow(cs).replace(Some(uart1));
    });

    loop {
        // Normal application logic
        free(|cs| {
            if let Some(uart) =
UART.borrow(cs).borrow_mut().as_mut() {
                // write to UART
            }
```

```
        });
    }
}

#[interrupt]
fn USART1_EXTI25() {
    free(|cs| {
        if let Some(uart) =
UART.borrow(cs).borrow_mut().as_mut() {
            // read from UART
        }
    });
}
```

This pattern avoids unsafe code and ensures that only one context accesses the UART peripheral at a time. It's a little verbose, but safe, and it's a good baseline when you're not using a higher-level concurrency model.

When to Use Atomics vs Mutexes

Use `Atomic*` types when:

The shared data is a primitive (bool, counter, flag)

The data fits in a single word and can be updated independently

You want low overhead and lock-free access

Use `Mutex<RefCell<>>` + `interrupt::free()` when:

The data is a struct, slice, or peripheral

You need to perform multiple reads/writes together

You want to ensure exclusive access across interrupt and non-interrupt contexts

Practical Exercise: Ring Buffer with Mutex

Here's a practical use case—logging UART bytes from an ISR into a ring buffer:

```
use heapless::spsc::Queue;
```

```rust
static RX_QUEUE: Mutex<RefCell<Option<Queue<u8,
64>>>> = Mutex::new(RefCell::new(None));

#[entry]
fn main() -> ! {
    free(|cs| {

RX_QUEUE.borrow(cs).replace(Some(Queue::new()));
    });

    loop {
        free(|cs| {
            if let Some(ref mut queue) =
RX_QUEUE.borrow(cs).borrow_mut().as_mut() {
                if let Some(byte) = queue.dequeue()
{
                    process(byte);
                }
            }
        });
    }
}

#[interrupt]
fn USART1_EXTI25() {
    free(|cs| {
        if let Some(ref mut queue) =
RX_QUEUE.borrow(cs).borrow_mut().as_mut() {
            if let Some(byte) = read_uart() {
                queue.enqueue(byte).ok();
            }
        }
    });
}
```

This pattern allows safe concurrent logging or buffering without corrupting memory or losing data, and heapless makes it easy to use fixed-size structures without dynamic allocation.

Synchronization in embedded Rust is not about adding locks—it's about designing your system to avoid unsafe access in the first place. Whether you're using atomics for fast counters or wrapping complex state in a Mutex, the goal

93

is the same: guarantee that data is accessed in a way that is **correct, exclusive, and race-free**.

Rust gives you the tools to express these constraints directly in your code, and the compiler enforces them for you. That means fewer surprises, safer firmware, and a much smoother development process when your software begins to grow.

Chapter 6: Peripherals and Communication Protocols

When your microcontroller talks to the outside world, it typically does so through communication protocols like UART, I2C, or SPI. These protocols let your embedded device send and receive data—whether you're printing debug logs over a serial port, reading temperature values from a digital sensor, or controlling an OLED display. Mastering these protocols is essential for writing real-world firmware that interacts with sensors, actuators, memory, displays, and other components.

Rust, through the `embedded-hal` trait system and microcontroller-specific HALs, gives you the power to work with these protocols in a safe, abstracted, and testable way. Whether you're reading a sensor over I2C or writing data to a flash chip via SPI, the patterns remain consistent, and the abstractions ensure correctness without compromising performance or control.

UART: Serial Communication in Rust

Serial communication is one of the most foundational tools in embedded systems development. It's typically the first feature you'll interact with when debugging firmware, monitoring system behavior, or talking to external modules like GPS devices, Wi-Fi chips, or microcontrollers. UART—short for Universal Asynchronous Receiver/Transmitter—is a simple two-wire communication protocol that transfers bytes in sequence, without needing a clock line. It's reliable, widespread, and supported by nearly every microcontroller.

UART communication is full-duplex, meaning it can send and receive simultaneously. It typically uses two lines:

TX (Transmit): sends data from the microcontroller to a connected device.

RX (Receive): reads data from the connected device into the microcontroller.

A UART peripheral is configured with several key parameters:

Baud rate (e.g., 9600, 115200): the speed at which bits are sent.

Data bits (typically 8)

Stop bits (usually 1)

Parity (none, even, or odd)

The UART hardware takes care of the bit-level transmission, start and stop bits, and synchronization. From your perspective as a developer, you're usually sending and receiving bytes or strings.

Setting Up UART with a HAL

Let's work through a real-world example using the `stm32f3xx-hal`, but this pattern is applicable to other microcontrollers like nRF, RP2040, or SAMD, as long as the corresponding HAL supports UART and the `embedded-hal` traits.

Here's how to configure UART to transmit data over USART1:

```rust
#![no_std]
#![no_main]

use cortex_m_rt::entry;
use panic_halt as _;

use stm32f3xx_hal::{
    pac,
    prelude::*,
    serial::{Serial, Tx},
};

use core::fmt::Write;

#[entry]
fn main() -> ! {
    let dp = pac::Peripherals::take().unwrap();
    let mut rcc = dp.RCC.constrain();
    let mut flash = dp.FLASH.constrain();

    let clocks = rcc.cfgr.freeze(&mut flash.acr);
    let mut gpioa = dp.GPIOA.split(&mut rcc.ahb);

    // Configure pins PA9 (TX) and PA10 (RX) to
    alternate function 7
```

```
    let tx = gpioa.pa9.into_af7(&mut gpioa.moder,
&mut gpioa.afrh);
    let rx = gpioa.pa10.into_af7(&mut gpioa.moder,
&mut gpioa.afrh);

    // Initialize USART1 with 115200 baud rate
    let serial = Serial::usart1(dp.USART1, (tx,
rx), 115_200.Bd(), clocks, &mut rcc.apb2);

    let (mut tx, _rx) = serial.split();

    // Send a message
    writeln!(tx, "UART is working!\r").unwrap();

    loop {
        // You could send periodic messages or echo
characters here
    }
}
```

Here's what this example does:

Configures the USART1 peripheral using the HAL

Maps the correct pins to their alternate functions

Sets a baud rate using `115_200.Bd()` (baud divisor helper)

Uses `writeln!()` to format and send a message over UART

The `writeln!` macro is available because the HAL implements `core::fmt::Write` for the TX half of the serial interface. This means you can use standard Rust formatting syntax (`{}`) to output formatted strings, which is incredibly useful for debugging or printing sensor values.

Receiving Data over UART

Sending data is straightforward. Receiving data takes a bit more care—especially when you want to do it without blocking the CPU. Let's start with the simplest way: blocking reads.

When you split the serial interface, the RX part supports `Read<u8>` from the embedded-hal trait. You can read one byte at a time using the `nb::block!` macro, which converts non-blocking behavior into a simple blocking call.

```
use embedded_hal::serial::Read;
use nb::block;

let received = block!(rx.read()).unwrap();
```

This works fine for simple scenarios, but it blocks execution while waiting for data. For more complex systems, you'll want to receive data in an interrupt-driven or DMA-based way, depending on your HAL's support.

Some HALs provide `listen()` and interrupt handlers for RX events:

```
serial.listen(Event::Rxne);

// In interrupt handler
#[interrupt]
fn USART1_EXTI25() {
    let byte = block!(rx.read()).unwrap();
    process(byte);
}
```

You can combine this with a ring buffer (like from the `heapless` crate) to store incoming data asynchronously.

Making a Reusable UART Logger

UART is most commonly used for logging and diagnostics. Instead of scattering `writeln!()` calls across your application, you can wrap the transmitter in a simple logger abstraction.

```
use embedded_hal::serial::Write;

pub struct Logger<TX>
where
    TX: Write<u8>,
{
    tx: TX,
}

impl<TX> Logger<TX>
```

```rust
where
    TX: Write<u8>,
{
    pub fn new(tx: TX) -> Self {
        Logger { tx }
    }

    pub fn log(&mut self, msg: &str) {
        for byte in msg.bytes() {
            nb::block!(self.tx.write(byte)).ok();
        }
    }
}
```

Then in `main()`:

```rust
let mut logger = Logger::new(tx);

logger.log("System initialized.\n");
```

This decouples your application from the serial details, and lets you test or extend your logger later—for instance, by adding timestamps or log levels.

Testing Serial Communication

To confirm that your UART is working:

Connect the board's TX pin to a USB-Serial adapter or a second microcontroller.

Use a serial terminal like `minicom`, `screen`, or `PuTTY` on your PC.

Match the baud rate (e.g., 115200) and disable flow control.

Power the board and observe the output.

You should see your log messages appear in the terminal. If nothing shows up, double-check:

Pin assignments (TX/RX must be correct and not reversed)

Alternate function configuration

Baud rate matching

99

Ground connection between devices

Common Pitfalls to Avoid

Using blocking reads in your main loop can halt your application if data never arrives. Use non-blocking reads or interrupt-based reception when building responsive systems.

Avoid `unwrap()` in production code—handle UART errors explicitly or use `.ok()` to discard them safely.

Make sure your TX and RX pins are routed correctly—many boards require manual pin configuration using GPIO alternate functions.

UART is a dependable and essential communication channel in embedded applications, and Rust gives you a clean, expressive, and safe way to use it. Whether you're sending logs, controlling an external module, or reading configuration commands, serial communication with UART gives your firmware visibility and flexibility.

By using HAL abstractions, implementing `embedded-hal` traits, and wrapping functionality in reusable interfaces, you can create UART-based features that are both portable and easy to integrate. As your project grows, UART will often remain your most valuable tool for diagnostics and control—so getting it right from the start pays off immediately.

I2C: Reading from Sensors

When you're building embedded systems that need to sense the environment—like monitoring temperature, pressure, humidity, or orientation—I2C is often the protocol you'll reach for. It's compact, relatively simple, and widely supported across thousands of sensors and integrated circuits. As a developer, your job is to send the right bytes to the right device and interpret the data it sends back. Rust makes this process safe, structured, and straightforward.

I2C (Inter-Integrated Circuit) is a synchronous, master-slave, multi-device bus protocol. It uses two wires:

SCL (Serial Clock Line): clock signal controlled by the master

SDA (Serial Data Line): bidirectional data line for sending and receiving bytes

Each device on the bus has a 7-bit address. The master initiates communication by sending the address of the device it wants to talk to, followed by either a read or write operation.

Common use cases:

Reading sensor values

Writing configuration registers

Communicating with EEPROMs or real-time clocks

Communication follows a sequence like:

Master sends the device address + write bit

Master sends register address to read from

Master sends the device address + read bit

Master reads one or more bytes

Let's see how this plays out in real embedded Rust code.

Setting Up I2C in Embedded Rust

We'll start with the `stm32f3xx-hal` crate, but the same structure applies across other HALs like `nrf-hal`, `atsamd-hal`, or `rp2040-hal`.

Here's how you configure I2C using PB6 as SCL and PB7 as SDA:

```
use stm32f3xx_hal::{pac, prelude::*, i2c::I2c};

#[entry]
fn main() -> ! {
    let dp = pac::Peripherals::take().unwrap();
    let mut rcc = dp.RCC.constrain();
    let clocks = rcc.cfgr.freeze(&mut
dp.FLASH.constrain().acr);
    let mut gpiob = dp.GPIOB.split(&mut rcc.ahb);

    // Configure I2C pins
```

```
    let scl = gpiob.pb6.into_af4(&mut gpiob.moder,
&mut gpiob.afrl);
    let sda = gpiob.pb7.into_af4(&mut gpiob.moder,
&mut gpiob.afrl);

    // Initialize I2C1 at 100kHz
    let mut i2c = I2c::i2c1(dp.I2C1, (scl, sda),
100.kHz(), clocks, &mut rcc.apb1);

    loop {
        // Sensor read logic here
    }
}
```

This sets up I2C1 on the STM32F3 series at 100 kHz—standard for many sensors.

Reading a Sensor Register

Most I2C sensors use a register-based interface. To read data:

You write the register address you want to read.

Then you read back a fixed number of bytes.

Here's how to read two bytes from register 0x00 on a sensor at address 0x48:

```
let address = 0x48;
let register = [0x00];
let mut buffer = [0; 2];

i2c.write_read(address, &register, &mut
buffer).unwrap();
```

This sends 0x00 to device 0x48, then reads two bytes into buffer.

Let's decode the result as a 12-bit temperature reading, common in devices like the TMP102:

```
let raw = ((buffer[0] as u16) << 8 | buffer[1] as
u16) >> 4;
let temperature_celsius = raw as f32 * 0.0625;
```

Now you've got a readable temperature value you can log or act on.

Building a Reusable Driver

To avoid repeating logic and hardcoding register offsets, wrap sensor interaction in a driver module. Here's a reusable driver for the TMP102 temperature sensor:

```rust
use embedded_hal::blocking::i2c::WriteRead;

pub struct Tmp102<I2C> {
    i2c: I2C,
    address: u8,
}

impl<I2C, E> Tmp102<I2C>
where
    I2C: WriteRead<Error = E>,
{
    pub fn new(i2c: I2C, address: u8) -> Self {
        Self { i2c, address }
    }

    pub fn read_temperature(&mut self) ->
Result<f32, E> {
        let mut buffer = [0; 2];
        self.i2c.write_read(self.address, &[0x00],
&mut buffer)?;

        let raw = ((buffer[0] as u16) << 8 |
buffer[1] as u16) >> 4;
        Ok(raw as f32 * 0.0625)
    }
}
```

Usage in your `main()` becomes clean and clear:

```rust
let mut sensor = Tmp102::new(i2c, 0x48);

let temp = sensor.read_temperature().unwrap();
```

This driver is hardware-independent. You can use it with any I2C peripheral that implements `WriteRead`, which makes it easy to test, reuse, and adapt across platforms.

Real-World Practice: Reading Periodically

You often want to sample sensor data on a fixed interval. Combine I2C reads with a timer:

```
loop {
    let temp = sensor.read_temperature().unwrap();
    log_temperature(temp);

    delay.delay_ms(1000u32);
}
```

In a production system, you'd probably replace `delay_ms` with a timer interrupt or RTIC task scheduled every second. But this pattern gets the job done when you're testing functionality.

Handling Errors Gracefully

I2C operations return a `Result`. This accounts for common issues like:

NACK from the device

Bus errors

Timeouts

Always handle these explicitly, especially in production code:

```
match sensor.read_temperature() {
    Ok(temp) => log(temp),
    Err(_) => log_error("Sensor not responding"),
}
```

You can also implement retry logic or watchdog resets if a sensor consistently fails.

Common Issues to Watch For

Incorrect address: Most sensor datasheets list a 7-bit address. Don't shift it left unless the HAL requires an 8-bit format.

No pull-ups: I2C lines must be pulled up with resistors (usually 4.7kΩ).

Crossed wires: SCL and SDA must be routed correctly.

Multiple masters: I2C supports multi-master setups, but these are uncommon and require careful arbitration logic.

I2C is the backbone of sensor communication in embedded systems. Whether you're measuring ambient conditions, monitoring hardware status, or collecting external input, chances are I2C will be involved.

With Rust and `embedded-hal`, you're equipped to work with I2C in a way that's both reliable and scalable. You can define clean interfaces, isolate hardware access, and avoid the boilerplate and bugs that often plague lower-level firmware.

SPI: Controlling Displays or Memory

SPI (Serial Peripheral Interface) is one of the fastest and most widely used protocols in embedded systems. If you've worked with OLED or TFT displays, SD cards, external flash memory, digital-to-analog converters, or even some wireless modules, there's a high chance they were connected via SPI. It's a straightforward, full-duplex protocol that relies on explicit clocking and precise timing.

Unlike I2C, SPI isn't address-based and doesn't support multiple devices sharing the same data lines unless you manage chip-select lines manually. But what it lacks in bus complexity, it makes up for in raw speed and simplicity. As a developer working with Rust and embedded HALs, your job is to configure the SPI peripheral correctly, manage chip select control, and handle data transactions cleanly and safely.

How SPI Works

SPI is a four-wire protocol:

SCLK (Serial Clock): driven by the master to control data timing

MOSI (Master Out Slave In): carries data from the master to the slave

MISO (Master In Slave Out): carries data from the slave to the master

CS (Chip Select): a manual line used by the master to activate one slave at a time

SPI is always master-driven: the master generates the clock and initiates every transfer. Each byte transfer is synchronous, meaning one bit is shifted out on MOSI for every bit read in on MISO, in parallel.

Every transaction requires:

A correctly configured SPI peripheral

Control over the CS pin (usually a GPIO output)

Correct SPI mode (clock polarity and phase) matching the target device

Configuring SPI in Rust with a HAL

We'll use the stm32f3xx-hal here, but again, the same structure applies to other microcontrollers supported by Rust.

Let's set up SPI1 with PA5 as SCLK, PA6 as MISO, and PA7 as MOSI:

```rust
use stm32f3xx_hal::{
    pac,
    prelude::*,
    spi::{Spi, Mode, Phase, Polarity},
};

#[entry]
fn main() -> ! {
    let dp = pac::Peripherals::take().unwrap();
    let mut rcc = dp.RCC.constrain();
    let clocks = rcc.cfgr.freeze(&mut
dp.FLASH.constrain().acr);
    let mut gpioa = dp.GPIOA.split(&mut rcc.ahb);

    // Configure SPI pins
    let sck = gpioa.pa5.into_af5(&mut gpioa.moder,
&mut gpioa.afrl);
    let miso = gpioa.pa6.into_af5(&mut gpioa.moder,
&mut gpioa.afrl);
    let mosi = gpioa.pa7.into_af5(&mut gpioa.moder,
&mut gpioa.afrl);

    // SPI mode: CPOL=0, CPHA=0 (Mode 0)
    let mode = Mode {
        polarity: Polarity::IdleLow,
```

```rust
        phase: Phase::CaptureOnFirstTransition,
    };

    let spi = Spi::spi1(
        dp.SPI1,
        (sck, miso, mosi),
        mode,
        8.mhz(),
        clocks,
        &mut rcc.apb2,
    );

    loop {
        // Your SPI logic here
    }
}
```

This initializes SPI1 in Mode 0 at 8 MHz. Most display controllers and flash chips support SPI mode 0 or 3, so always confirm this in the device's datasheet before setting up the mode.

Sending and Receiving Data

SPI in Rust typically uses the `Write` or `Transfer` traits from `embedded-hal`. For example, to send a command to a flash memory device or display controller:

```rust
use embedded_hal::blocking::spi::Write;

let mut data = [0x9F]; // Example: Read JEDEC ID
command
spi.write(&data).unwrap();
```

If the device returns data, you'll need to use `transfer()`:

```rust
use embedded_hal::blocking::spi::Transfer;

let mut buffer = [0x9F, 0x00, 0x00, 0x00]; //
Command + empty bytes for read
spi.transfer(&mut buffer).unwrap();

// The buffer now contains: [0x9F, ID1, ID2, ID3]
```

SPI is full-duplex. That means even when you're just writing, the peripheral will simultaneously read bytes (usually garbage unless you're expecting input). This is why `transfer()` replaces the buffer contents with received bytes, and `write()` ignores incoming data.

Controlling the Chip Select (CS) Pin

Most SPI devices need their CS pin to be driven low during communication. This is almost always handled manually using a regular GPIO configured as output:

```
let mut cs = gpioa.pa4.into_push_pull_output(&mut
gpioa.moder, &mut gpioa.otyper);

cs.set_low().unwrap();      // Begin SPI transaction
spi.write(&[0x06]).unwrap(); // Send some command
cs.set_high().unwrap();     // End SPI transaction
```

Timing around CS matters. Some devices latch commands or data on rising or falling edges, so ensure CS is properly toggled before and after each transfer.

Talking to an SPI Flash Chip

Let's read the JEDEC ID of an SPI flash device. This is a good sanity check to confirm that SPI wiring, logic level, and command format are working.

```
let mut cs = gpioa.pa4.into_push_pull_output(&mut
gpioa.moder, &mut gpioa.otyper);

let mut buffer = [0x9F, 0, 0, 0]; // Read JEDEC ID
command

cs.set_low().unwrap();
spi.transfer(&mut buffer).unwrap();
cs.set_high().unwrap();

let manufacturer_id = buffer[1];
let memory_type = buffer[2];
let capacity = buffer[3];
```

Each SPI device has its own command set, so refer to the datasheet. The example above works for most SPI NOR flash chips (like the W25Q series).

Controlling a Display with SPI

Many graphical displays—like OLEDs or small color TFTs—use SPI. Libraries like embedded-graphics and display-interface-spi integrate with Rust HALs to provide a high-level API.

Here's a basic usage outline:

```
use display_interface_spi::SPIInterfaceNoCS;
use ssd1306::{prelude::*, Ssd1306};

let interface = SPIInterfaceNoCS::new(spi, dc);
let mut display = Ssd1306::new(interface,
DisplaySize128x64, DisplayRotation::Rotate0)
    .into_buffered_graphics_mode();

display.init().unwrap();
display.clear();
display.flush().unwrap();
```

In this example:

dc is a Data/Command control pin

spi is your SPI peripheral

display is a driver for an SSD1306 OLED screen

This level of abstraction lets you draw text, shapes, or bitmaps on the display without worrying about individual SPI commands.

Designing Reusable SPI Drivers

Let's say you're building a driver for a digital potentiometer or DAC over SPI. You can abstract the SPI interface using embedded-hal traits so that your code is portable across HALs:

```
use embedded_hal::blocking::spi::Write;
use embedded_hal::digital::v2::OutputPin;

pub struct MySpiDevice<SPI, CS> {
    spi: SPI,
    cs: CS,
}
```

```
impl<SPI, CS, E> MySpiDevice<SPI, CS>
where
    SPI: Write<u8, Error = E>,
    CS: OutputPin,
{
    pub fn new(spi: SPI, cs: CS) -> Self {
        Self { spi, cs }
    }

    pub fn write_register(&mut self, addr: u8,
value: u8) -> Result<(), E> {
        let packet = [addr, value];
        self.cs.set_low().ok();
        let result = self.spi.write(&packet);
        self.cs.set_high().ok();
        result
    }
}
```

You can now use this driver with any microcontroller that provides an SPI interface. This approach promotes reuse and consistency across platforms.

Troubleshooting Tips

No response: Check CS timing, SPI mode, and data polarity.

Wrong data: Verify byte order (big-endian vs little-endian) and bit significance.

Clock too fast: Many devices require a slow initial clock (100 kHz or 1 MHz) during startup.

No display activity: If using a graphical display, confirm dc, reset, and initialization sequence.

SPI offers a fast and efficient way to talk to devices that need high-speed data transfer or don't fit well with slower protocols like I2C. Whether you're communicating with a display, a memory chip, or a DAC, SPI gives you direct, predictable control over how and when data moves.

Rust's abstractions make it easy to work with SPI safely—wrapping volatile byte transfers in expressive types, managing chip select lines with clean control, and supporting a hardware-agnostic design through `embedded-hal`. These patterns allow you to scale from small SPI commands to large, reusable drivers, all while retaining safety and clarity in your firmware.

Writing Reusable Peripheral Drivers

When working with sensors, displays, memory chips, or other hardware components, you don't want to rewrite logic for every microcontroller you use. What you want is a clean driver—a module or struct that encapsulates all the communication details and presents a simple interface to the rest of your application. And most importantly, you want that driver to be reusable.

Reusable peripheral drivers are at the core of reliable embedded development. They make your code more maintainable, easier to test, and portable across devices. In Rust, the key to writing reusable drivers lies in abstraction: you use traits from `embedded-hal` to describe the communication interface generically, so your driver can work with any hardware that implements those traits—whether you're on an STM32, RP2040, or a virtual mock for testing.

In embedded C, drivers often rely on low-level register manipulation or chip-specific headers. This tightly couples the driver to a specific microcontroller. Rust does the opposite: by building on `embedded-hal` traits like `Write`, `Read`, and `WriteRead`, you separate your driver logic from the hardware. This means:

You can use the same sensor driver on different boards.

You can swap hardware without touching your driver.

You can write unit tests using fake or mock implementations of the hardware interface.

You don't write for "the STM32 I2C peripheral"—you write for anything that implements `embedded_hal::blocking::i2c::WriteRead`.

Let's now walk through building such a driver.

Case Study: TMP102 Temperature Sensor (I2C)

The TMP102 is a common digital temperature sensor. It uses I2C and returns 12-bit temperature values. To get the current temperature:

You send register address `0x00`.

You read back two bytes.

You convert the value into degrees Celsius.

Here's a reusable Rust driver for this sensor:

```rust
use embedded_hal::blocking::i2c::WriteRead;

pub struct Tmp102<I2C> {
    i2c: I2C,
    address: u8,
}

impl<I2C, E> Tmp102<I2C>
where
    I2C: WriteRead<Error = E>,
{
    pub fn new(i2c: I2C, address: u8) -> Self {
        Self { i2c, address }
    }

    pub fn read_temperature(&mut self) ->
Result<f32, E> {
        let mut buffer = [0u8; 2];
        self.i2c.write_read(self.address, &[0x00],
&mut buffer)?;

        let raw = ((buffer[0] as u16) << 8 |
buffer[1] as u16) >> 4;
        Ok(raw as f32 * 0.0625)
    }

    pub fn release(self) -> I2C {
        self.i2c
    }
}
```

This driver:

Is generic over any type `I2C` that implements the `WriteRead` trait.

Can be used with any HAL's I2C implementation.

Does not depend on any specific board or MCU.

Can be unit tested with a mock I2C interface.

You use this driver like so:

```
let i2c = I2c::i2c1(...); // HAL-specific setup
let mut sensor = Tmp102::new(i2c, 0x48);

let temp = sensor.read_temperature().unwrap();
```

This is clean, safe, and universal.

SPI-Based Device Driver Example

Let's take a look at a generic SPI driver—for example, an SPI DAC or digital potentiometer.

Here's how you might implement a reusable driver for a device with a simple register-write interface:

```
use embedded_hal::blocking::spi::Write;
use embedded_hal::digital::v2::OutputPin;

pub struct SpiDevice<SPI, CS> {
    spi: SPI,
    cs: CS,
}

impl<SPI, CS, E> SpiDevice<SPI, CS>
where
    SPI: Write<u8, Error = E>,
    CS: OutputPin,
{
    pub fn new(spi: SPI, cs: CS) -> Self {
        Self { spi, cs }
    }

    pub fn write_register(&mut self, addr: u8,
value: u8) -> Result<(), E> {
        let packet = [addr, value];
        self.cs.set_low().ok(); // Begin
transaction
        let result = self.spi.write(&packet);
```

```
        self.cs.set_high().ok(); // End transaction
        result
    }
}
```

This driver accepts any SPI bus and CS pin that implement the appropriate traits. It works on all HALs that follow embedded-hal.

To use this driver:

```
let spi = Spi::spi1(...);
let cs = gpioa.pa4.into_push_pull_output(...);

let mut device = SpiDevice::new(spi, cs);
device.write_register(0x01, 0x7F).unwrap();
```

Your SPI logic is now abstracted and reusable.

Generic UART Logger Driver

For UART, you often want a simple logger. Here's a serial writer driver that supports formatted messages using the standard core::fmt::Write trait.

```
use embedded_hal::serial::Write;
use nb::block;

pub struct Logger<TX> {
    tx: TX,
}

impl<TX> Logger<TX>
where
    TX: Write<u8>,
{
    pub fn new(tx: TX) -> Self {
        Self { tx }
    }

    pub fn send_str(&mut self, msg: &str) {
        for b in msg.as_bytes() {
            block!(self.tx.write(*b)).ok();
        }
    }
```

```
}
```

Use it like this:

```
let serial = Serial::usart1(...);
let (mut tx, _rx) = serial.split();
let mut logger = Logger::new(tx);

logger.send_str("Starting up...\n");
```

You can also implement `core::fmt::Write` for `Logger` and use `write!()`
macros:

```
impl<TX> core::fmt::Write for Logger<TX>
where
    TX: Write<u8>,
{
    fn write_str(&mut self, s: &str) ->
core::fmt::Result {
        for b in s.bytes() {
            block!(self.tx.write(b)).map_err(|_|
core::fmt::Error)?;
        }
        Ok(())
    }
}
```

Now you can write:

```
writeln!(logger, "Voltage: {:.2}V",
voltage).unwrap();
```

Testing and Mocking Drivers

Reusable drivers can be tested using **mocks**—fake implementations of the
I2C, SPI, or UART traits.

Use `embedded-hal-mock` for mocking hardware in unit tests:

```
[dev-dependencies]

embedded-hal-mock = "0.9.0"
```

Example test for the TMP102 driver:

115

```rust
use embedded_hal_mock::i2c::{Mock as I2cMock,
Transaction as I2cTrans};
use your_crate::Tmp102;

#[test]
fn reads_temperature_correctly() {
    let expectations = [I2cTrans::write_read(0x48,
vec![0x00], vec![0x7D, 0x00])];
    let mut i2c = I2cMock::new(&expectations);

    let mut sensor = Tmp102::new(i2c.clone(),
0x48);
    let temp = sensor.read_temperature().unwrap();

    assert_eq!(temp, 125.0);
    i2c.done(); // Assert all expectations were met
}
```

This lets you test driver logic on your development machine without needing hardware.

Best Practices for Driver Design

Accept generic parameters that implement embedded-hal traits

Avoid storing platform-specific types inside your driver

Keep your driver focused on one component

Provide a clear public interface (e.g., `read_temperature()`, `set_output(value)`)

Always provide a way to release the interface (e.g., a `.release()` method that returns the I2C or SPI bus)

These patterns ensure your drivers are portable, composable, and easy to debug.

Reusable peripheral drivers are the building blocks of embedded system design. They allow you to separate hardware control from business logic, promote portability, and simplify testing. In Rust, by building on `embedded-hal` traits, you create abstractions that are safe, structured, and highly adaptable—fitting seamlessly into your firmware across boards and product generations.

With UART, I2C, and SPI under your belt, and a deep understanding of how to write hardware-agnostic drivers, you're now equipped to build embedded software that is professional-grade, easy to maintain, and ready for scaling across devices.

Chapter 7: Power Efficiency and Sleep Modes

In embedded systems, performance is important—but efficiency is what often defines the success of your design. Whether you're building a wearable device, a battery-powered sensor, or a solar-powered data logger, managing power effectively is critical. If your microcontroller spends most of its time running at full speed doing nothing, you're wasting precious energy. Fortunately, most microcontrollers support multiple sleep modes and power optimization features designed exactly for this.

This chapter will walk you through the fundamentals of embedded power management and show you how to use sleep modes and low-power strategies in Rust. You'll learn how to configure your system to enter sleep states, wake up from interrupts, measure power consumption, and write code that respects the constraints of battery-powered deployments—all with clear examples and actionable patterns you can apply to your own hardware.

Embedded Power Management Principles

In embedded systems, power is not just a constraint—it's often a core design priority. Whether you're building a battery-powered sensor node, a wearable health tracker, or an industrial controller with strict power budgets, your application needs to make the most of every microamp. To do that, you have to design your firmware and hardware to minimize unnecessary activity and avoid waste.

Power management is about structuring your system to stay asleep as much as possible, operate only when it needs to, and keep everything that's not being used completely turned off. It's a discipline that affects how you structure code, how you choose peripherals, and how you configure the microcontroller's internal systems. Let's unpack how that works in practice.

At the start of any low-power project, you want to ask: **What is the system's job?** Then: **How often does it really need to be awake to do that job?** Most embedded applications don't need to be awake all the time. They typically:

Sample a sensor every few seconds or minutes

Send data occasionally

Wake up on external triggers like a button press or GPIO interrupt

Once you identify those events, you structure your firmware around them. The goal is to sleep in between, only wake when necessary, and go back to sleep immediately after.

For example, a temperature logger that samples every 10 seconds and sends data once a minute could spend over 99% of its time in a deep sleep mode. If you're not explicitly using that sleep time, you're burning power unnecessarily.

Power Domains and Microcontroller Features

Most modern microcontrollers have several internal **power domains**—groups of logic blocks and peripherals that can be turned off independently. You can often disable:

Unused clocks (for buses and peripherals)

Entire communication blocks like SPI or UART

ADCs, timers, or USB controllers

Even sections of SRAM or flash interface logic

When you reduce clock domains or disable peripheral blocks, the microcontroller stops drawing current from them. These savings add up quickly, especially in systems that operate continuously over long periods.

On the STM32 family, for example, the RCC (Reset and Clock Control) peripheral lets you enable or disable individual clock gates:

```
dp.RCC.apb1enr.modify(|_, w|
w.tim2en().clear_bit()); // Disable TIM2
```

You should do this as soon as you know a peripheral is not needed. Similarly, before entering a low-power mode, disable peripherals that were only needed during active computation.

Run, Sleep, Stop, Standby: Modes Explained

Microcontrollers typically support several **power modes**, ranging from full speed to ultra-low power. Here's how to think about them:

Run Mode: CPU and all peripherals are active. This is the highest current state, but necessary for work.

Sleep Mode: The CPU clock is stopped, but peripheral clocks can continue. You use this when waiting for an interrupt (like UART RX or timer) without needing CPU computation.

Stop Mode (or Deep Sleep): All high-speed clocks are stopped. The CPU, most peripherals, and the system clock halt, but some wake-up sources remain active—like RTC alarms or external interrupts.

Standby Mode: Almost everything is off. Only a minimal wake-up logic remains, and often no RAM is retained. Use this for deep hibernation between infrequent tasks.

You select the right mode depending on how soon the system needs to wake up and how much state you need to retain.

In Rust (for Cortex-M), you enter sleep with:

```
use cortex_m::asm;

asm::wfi(); // Wait For Interrupt
```

This halts the core but allows it to resume instantly on interrupt.

For deeper sleep modes, you configure system control and power registers:

```
let scb =
cortex_m::peripheral::SCB::borrow_unchecked();

scb.set_sleepdeep();

asm::wfi();
```

Make sure your wake-up logic is configured before entering sleep. Otherwise, the system may not recover until reset.

Interrupt-Driven Design Is Essential

Low-power systems cannot rely on polling loops. Busy-waiting consumes CPU cycles and wastes energy. Instead, restructure your application around **interrupts**:

Use a timer interrupt instead of polling `millis()`

Enable GPIO interrupts for button presses

Use DMA with a completion interrupt instead of manually moving data

For example, rather than checking for UART input in a loop:

```
loop {
    if uart.rx_ready() {
        let byte = uart.read();
        process(byte);
    }
}
```

You use:

```
#[interrupt]
fn USART1() {
    let byte = uart.read();
    process(byte);
}
```

This way, your main loop can enter sleep immediately and stay there until the UART interrupt fires.

Use Timers to Structure Wakeups

Most ultra-low-power systems use a hardware timer to wake the device after a period of inactivity. This can be a general-purpose timer or a dedicated RTC.

On STM32, for example:

```
dp.RTC.cr.modify(|_, w| w.wute().set_bit()); //
Enable wake-up timer
```

You configure the timer to trigger an interrupt every few seconds or minutes. Inside that interrupt, you read sensors, process data, and then go right back to sleep.

This pattern ensures that your active time is predictable and limited.

Peripherals Draw Power Too

Even when the CPU is asleep, peripherals may continue running. This can be helpful (e.g., when using timers or UART RX), but can also consume power unnecessarily.

You should disable:

SPI/UART/I2C blocks when inactive

ADC or DAC if not actively converting

USB when not connected

Internal regulators or boost converters for unneeded voltages

For example, if you're using UART only occasionally:

```
serial.disable(); // HAL-specific function, or
disable clock gate directly
```

Every peripheral you turn off can reduce idle current dramatically.

GPIO Configuration Matters

Unused GPIOs can cause leakage or power spikes if left floating. Best practice:

Set unused pins as outputs and drive them low

Avoid leaving high-speed alternate functions active

Disable pull-ups and pull-downs unless explicitly needed

On STM32, configure unused pins in reset state or:

```
gpioa.pa3.into_push_pull_output(&mut    gpioa.moder,    &mut
gpioa.otyper).set_low().ok();
```

For ultra-low-power modes, you may also need to disable debug pins like SWD or JTAG, which can keep the system awake due to pull-up resistors and clocking.

Power-efficient firmware is built by design, not by accident. You need to understand your microcontroller's modes, use its low-power features purposefully, and restructure your code around interrupts and events instead of loops and polling.

In embedded Rust, you have full access to the control registers, and you can express sleep transitions and peripheral configuration safely and clearly. That gives you the tools to build systems that run longer, cooler, and smarter—with less code and greater reliability.

Configuring Sleep and Wake-Up Logic

Once you understand how power modes work, the next step is to integrate them into your firmware structure so that your microcontroller sleeps when it should and wakes up exactly when it's supposed to. This isn't just about calling `wfi()` and hoping for the best—it's about carefully configuring which peripherals, interrupts, and timers can bring the system back to life after it's gone to sleep.

Your system should treat active processing as the exception, not the default. The normal state should be sleeping or stopped, and when something important happens—a button is pressed, a timer expires, a byte arrives on UART—that's when the system wakes up, processes the event, and immediately returns to a low-power state.

Putting the CPU to Sleep

At the simplest level, you put the CPU into sleep mode using the `cortex-m` crate:

```
use cortex_m::asm;

loop {
    asm::wfi(); // Wait For Interrupt
}
```

This halts the CPU core until the next interrupt occurs. Peripherals continue running (if their clocks are active), and any interrupt can wake the system. You resume exactly where you left off—this is a core-safe instruction and typically consumes far less current than active run mode.

But to go deeper—such as STOP or STANDBY modes—you need to do more than just call `wfi()`.

Configuring Deep Sleep (STOP or STANDBY Modes)

Most microcontrollers include flags to distinguish between regular sleep and deep sleep modes. On Cortex-M devices, this is done through the System Control Block (SCB):

```
let scb =
cortex_m::peripheral::SCB::borrow_unchecked();

scb.set_sleepdeep();
```

Once `SLEEPDEEP` is set, the next `wfi()` or `wfe()` instruction sends the device into deep sleep instead of regular sleep. On STM32, this corresponds to STOP or STANDBY depending on how the power control registers are configured.

For STM32 STOP mode, for example:

```
let pwr = dp.PWR;

pwr.cr.modify(|_, w| w.lpds().set_bit()); // Low-
power deep sleep
```

This configuration tells the device to enter STOP mode when the CPU goes to sleep. Now, you just need to decide what wakes it up.

Enabling Wake-Up Sources

To return from sleep, your microcontroller needs to be told what to listen for. This could be:

A timer (RTC, SysTick, or general-purpose timer)

A GPIO pin (rising/falling edge on a button or signal line)

A communication event (e.g., UART RX)

Let's go over each of these with code examples.

Waking Up with a Timer (RTC or SysTick)

A low-power timer or RTC is perfect for periodic wake-ups. Let's say you want to wake up every 5 seconds to read a sensor. First, configure the RTC or timer to generate a periodic interrupt.

```
// Example: using the RTC wake-up timer (STM32)

dp.RTC.wutr.write(|w| unsafe { w.wut().bits(0xF000)
}); // Set timeout value

dp.RTC.cr.modify(|_, w| w.wutie().set_bit()); //
Enable wake-up interrupt

dp.RTC.cr.modify(|_, w| w.wute().set_bit());  //
Enable the timer


dp.SCB.set_sleepdeep(); // Configure deep sleep

cortex_m::asm::wfi();    // Sleep until RTC fires
```

Then, define an interrupt handler:

```
#[interrupt]
fn RTC_WKUP() {
    // Clear interrupt flag
    dp.RTC.isr.modify(|_, w| w.wutf().clear_bit());

    // Handle wake-up logic
    let temperature = read_sensor();
    store_or_send_data(temperature);
}
```

This pattern is ideal for data loggers, remote sensors, or anything that needs to perform a task at regular intervals without staying awake.

Waking Up from GPIO (External Interrupts)

If you want your system to wake when a button is pressed or a signal changes on a pin, configure an EXTI (external interrupt).

Example: wake from GPIO pin PA0 on a rising edge.

```
// Enable SYSCFG and EXTI line for PA0
```

```
dp.SYSCFG.exticr1.modify(|_, w| unsafe {
w.exti0().bits(0b0000) }); // Map EXTI0 to PA0
dp.EXTI.imr.modify(|_, w| w.mr0().set_bit()); //
Unmask EXTI0
dp.EXTI.rtsr.modify(|_, w| w.tr0().set_bit()); //
Rising edge trigger

// Optionally enable NVIC interrupt
unsafe {

cortex_m::peripheral::NVIC::unmask(pac::Interrupt::
EXTI0);
}
```

Then, in the interrupt handler:

```
#[interrupt]
fn EXTI0() {
    dp.EXTI.pr.write(|w| w.pr0().set_bit()); //
Clear pending flag

    // Wake-up task logic here
    handle_button_press();
}
```

And finally, sleep:

```
dp.SCB.set_sleepdeep();

cortex_m::asm::wfi();
```

This lets the system stay asleep until the user takes an action or a device signals readiness.

UART Wake-Up on RX Activity

UART wake-up is especially useful when your device receives data sporadically. Most HALs don't expose direct wake-on-RX configuration, so you'll work at the register level.

For STM32, configure the USART to trigger an interrupt on RXNE (Receive Not Empty):

```
dp.USART1.cr1.modify(|_, w| w.rxneie().set_bit());
// Enable RX interrupt
```

Now, enter sleep:

```
dp.SCB.clear_sleepdeep(); // Only light sleep
required

cortex_m::asm::wfi();
```

Handle the received data in your interrupt:

```
#[interrupt]
fn USART1_EXTI25() {
    let byte = dp.USART1.rdr.read().rdr().bits() as
u8;
    process_byte(byte);
}
```

This structure allows the CPU to stay halted until a character comes in, saving CPU cycles while still responding quickly.

Post-Wake Handling: Reset or Resume

When the system wakes up from sleep, it resumes **exactly where it left off** unless you've entered Standby mode. In Standby, the system often resets on wake-up, and you need to check special flags to know why the system restarted.

Example (STM32 check for Standby wake):

```
let woke_from_standby = dp.PWR.csr.read().sbf().bit_is_set();
```

You can conditionally branch on this to handle initialization differently on fresh boot vs. wake-up.

In STOP mode, however, RAM contents are retained. You can continue using data in memory without reinitialization, which is perfect for applications that maintain buffers or session state.

Example: Periodic Temperature Logger

Let's combine everything: your system should wake every 30 seconds, read temperature, store it, and go back to sleep.

Configure RTC for 30-second wakeup.

Put system into STOP mode.

On interrupt, read sensor and go back to sleep.

```
loop {
    dp.SCB.set_sleepdeep();
    cortex_m::asm::wfi(); // Wait for RTC

    let temp = read_temp_sensor();
    store_in_memory(temp);
}
```

In your `RTC_WKUP` interrupt, just clear the flag. The logic runs in the main loop post-wakeup.

Sleep and wake-up logic is the foundation of building embedded applications that are power-aware, event-driven, and capable of long operation on limited energy. By planning ahead and tying your system's activity to specific wake events, you reduce idle cycles, save power, and make your application more predictable.

In Rust, you do all of this explicitly and safely. You configure your interrupts with care, manage power modes through register access or HAL calls, and structure your application around events—not loops. With the right setup, your microcontroller can sleep for seconds, minutes, or even hours—yet be ready to act instantly when needed.

Measuring and Reducing Power Consumption

Knowing how much power your embedded system consumes—and why—is essential when building anything that runs on limited energy. Whether it's powered by a coin cell, a rechargeable lithium battery, or harvested solar energy, you must understand what's drawing current at every moment, and how you can optimize that without compromising functionality.

There's no guesswork here. You need hard measurements, careful system observation, and a set of reliable techniques to systematically reduce power usage. This section will guide you through the right way to measure

128

consumption, interpret the numbers you get, and apply real firmware techniques—using embedded Rust—that result in real savings.

Why Measuring Power Is Non-Negotiable

Before you can optimize anything, you need data. Measuring current consumption shows you:

Whether your sleep modes are working

Which parts of your firmware are drawing power

How much energy is consumed per operation

Whether there are leaks, clock misconfigurations, or active peripherals left on

You may have configured STOP mode correctly, but if a clock gate is still open or a peripheral isn't disabled, your current draw might be 10x what you expect.

Measurement allows you to validate that your firmware and hardware work together efficiently.

How to Measure Current Consumption

There are a few effective ways to measure current in embedded systems. Your choice depends on your tools and the resolution you need.

1. USB Current Monitors

Basic devices like the UM25C or Power-Z meters plug between your USB power supply and the development board. They give you live readings of current and voltage.

They're fine for rough measurements but lack the resolution to catch deep sleep behavior, where current might drop below 100μA.

2. Shunt Resistor + Multimeter

Place a precision resistor (e.g., 1Ω or 10Ω) in series with the power line. Measure the voltage drop across it to calculate current:

```
Current (A) = Voltage (V) / Resistance (Ω)
```

This is simple, accurate, and works well when measuring sleep and active phases with a DMM. Use low-resistance precision shunts (0.1Ω to 10Ω) depending on your expected current range.

3. Power Profiler Tools

Devices like the Nordic Power Profiler Kit II or Joulescope offer much higher resolution and sampling rates. These let you capture:

Sleep current down to microamps

Wake transitions in milliseconds

Current draw during specific code execution

They connect to your PC, record traces, and let you correlate current draw with code activity—ideal for detailed analysis.

Measuring Sleep vs Active Current

To measure correctly, isolate each mode:

For **sleep current**, ensure no interrupts are firing and leave the system in STOP or STANDBY mode for several seconds. Record the steady-state current.

For **active current**, trigger an event (e.g., timer interrupt) and observe the current during processing. Then return to sleep and confirm that the current drops back down.

Here's an example cycle:

System sleeps for 10 seconds (~5µA)

Wakes, samples sensor (~5mA for 50ms)

Sleeps again

Over time, you can calculate energy used per cycle:

```
Energy = Current × Voltage × Time
```

This lets you estimate battery life based on usage patterns.

Reducing Power Consumption in Practice

Now that you're measuring, let's talk about actions. Start by asking: **what's using power unnecessarily?**

1. Disable Unused Peripherals

Every peripheral uses some energy—especially analog components (ADC, DAC), clocks, and communication interfaces. Disable them when not needed:

```
dp.RCC.apb1enr.modify(|_, w|
w.tim2en().clear_bit()); // Disable TIM2
```

In Rust, your HAL may expose `.disable()` or `.release()` methods, or you can directly clear clock enable bits using PAC access.

2. Turn Off GPIO Outputs and Floating Pins

Even a few floating or active GPIOs can add hundreds of microamps.

Set unused pins to `Analog` mode (low leakage)

Drive outputs low if not used

Disable internal pull-ups/pull-downs where not needed

```
gpioa.pa3.into_analog(&mut gpioa.moder, &mut gpioa.pupdr);
```

This configures PA3 in analog mode with no pull resistors—minimizing leakage.

3. Reduce Clock Frequency

The system clock controls how fast your CPU and peripherals run. Lower frequencies mean lower dynamic power. For STM32:

```
let clocks = rcc.cfgr.sysclk(2.mhz()).freeze(&mut
flash.acr);
```

You can run at full speed when active, but reduce to 2 MHz or lower during idle processing or communication delays.

4. Minimize CPU Wake Time

Every millisecond the CPU is awake burns power. Keep active routines short:

Sample sensors quickly and use DMA if available

Process and compress data efficiently

Transmit only necessary bytes

Then return to sleep:

```
use cortex_m::asm;

asm::wfi(); // Return to low-power mode
```

5. Use Wake Timers Instead of Polling

Polling is wasteful. Use timer interrupts to structure periodic tasks.

```
#[interrupt]
fn RTC_WKUP() {
    let reading = read_sensor();
    transmit(reading);
    prepare_sleep(); // Configure STOP mode again
}
```

This replaces long polling loops with short bursts of activity.

6. Use DMA for Transfers

Direct Memory Access (DMA) lets you move data between peripherals and memory without waking the CPU. If your HAL supports it, configure DMA for SPI, UART, or ADC transfers.

This can reduce active time significantly and eliminate CPU-bound loops.

Verifying Optimization Success

After each optimization:

Re-measure current draw

Validate wake-up behavior still works

Confirm peripherals still behave as expected

Test in real conditions (battery, field environment, RF noise, etc.)

Track your active vs sleep current and update your energy budget model.

For example:

Active: 5mA for 100ms every 10s = 5mA * 0.1s = 0.5mAs every 10s

Sleep: 10µA for 9.9s = 0.00001A * 9.9s = 0.099mAs

Total per cycle: 0.599mAs

Daily usage = (8640 cycles/day) × 0.599mAs ≈ 5.17As/day

Then calculate battery life based on capacity.

Efficient embedded systems don't just work—they work **responsibly**, using only the power they truly need. Measuring power consumption is not optional. It's a continuous part of development, right alongside debugging and testing.

Rust's explicit control over hardware access, paired with safe HAL abstractions and low-level register access via PACs, gives you the best of both worlds. You can optimize deeply—down to every peripheral and pin—while keeping your code clean, structured, and predictable.

Writing Battery-Friendly Applications

If your embedded device is expected to run on battery, you're not just writing firmware—you're designing around energy. Your application's behavior directly determines how long the battery lasts, whether it dies early under certain conditions, and how often it needs to be recharged or replaced. Writing battery-friendly firmware means taking full control of when and how often the microcontroller wakes, what peripherals are active at any given time, how long tasks run, and how efficiently data is handled.

Before you optimize code, think through your application's job. What exactly does it need to do, and when?

Let's say you're building a soil moisture sensor:

It only needs to take one reading every 10 minutes.

It only transmits if the reading is different from the last one or crosses a threshold.

It should sleep the rest of the time.

That means:

The CPU needs to be awake for a few milliseconds every 10 minutes.

The ADC only needs to power up briefly.

The radio can be off unless a transmission is required.

You reduce power not just by lowering current, but by shortening **on-time** and **reducing how often tasks run**. This shift in mindset is key.

Use Low-Duty Cycle Task Scheduling

Let's structure the example using Rust and the RTIC framework:

```rust
#[rtic::app(device = stm32f3xx_hal::pac,
peripherals = true)]
mod app {
    use super::*;
    use cortex_m::asm;
    use stm32f3xx_hal::{prelude::*, rtc::Rtc,
adc::Adc};

    #[shared]
    struct Shared {}

    #[local]
    struct Local {
        adc: Adc<pac::ADC1>,
    }

    #[init]
    fn init(ctx: init::Context) -> (Shared, Local,
init::Monotonics()) {
        // Setup code for clocks, GPIOs, ADC, RTC,
etc.

        schedule_next_sample().unwrap();
        (Shared {}, Local { adc },
init::Monotonics())
    }

    #[task(local = [adc])]
    fn sample_moisture(ctx:
sample_moisture::Context) {
        let value =
ctx.local.adc.read(&moisture_pin).unwrap();
```

```
        if value > THRESHOLD {
            transmit_data(value);
        }

        schedule_next_sample().unwrap();
    }

    fn schedule_next_sample() -> Result<(), ()> {
sample_moisture::spawn_after(10.minutes()).map_err(
|_| ())
    }
}
```

The application:

Sleeps by default.

Wakes on a scheduled event.

Performs a fast measurement.

Sends data only when needed.

Goes straight back to sleep.

This is the architecture you want. Nothing runs unless it has to.

Minimize Peripheral On-Time

Battery-friendly applications power peripherals **only when needed**. Leaving them on is wasteful—even if the CPU is asleep.

Example: ADC

```
let mut adc = Adc::adc1(dp.ADC1, clocks, &mut
rcc.ahb);
adc.enable();

let sample = adc.read(&pin).unwrap();

adc.disable();
```

Always disable or release peripherals immediately after use.

135

This applies to:

UARTs

SPI/I2C

ADC/DAC

Timers

Internal voltage references

Your HAL may expose `.release()` or `.disable()`—use them. If not, access the registers via PAC and clear the enable bit manually.

Reduce Data Transmission Frequency

Wireless data transfer (BLE, LoRa, WiFi) often consumes far more power than computation. You can extend battery life dramatically by:

Sending less often

Sending only if the data changes

Compressing payloads

Using acknowledgment-based batching

In Rust, you can track the previous sensor value and only transmit if there's a significant delta:

```
static mut LAST_VALUE: u16 = 0;

fn should_transmit(new: u16) -> bool {
    let old = unsafe { LAST_VALUE };
    if (new as i32 - old as i32).abs() > 5 {
        unsafe { LAST_VALUE = new; }
        true
    } else {
        false
    }
}
```

Then call `should_transmit(value)` before using the radio.

This pattern—**event-based transmission**—saves energy without losing meaningful data.

Scale Performance Dynamically

If your microcontroller supports dynamic clock scaling (often via the RCC or PWR control registers), you can reduce clock frequency when not under load:

```
let clocks = rcc.cfgr.sysclk(2.mhz()).freeze(&mut
flash.acr);
```

If you need a burst of performance (e.g., during computation or radio use), bump the clock up:

```
let clocks = rcc.cfgr.sysclk(16.mhz()).freeze(&mut
flash.acr);
```

Then reduce it again afterward.

Some systems even scale voltage with frequency. This gives you a second level of savings—lowering core voltage reduces static current.

If dynamic scaling isn't available, you can still **configure a lower default frequency** during initialization.

Handle Low Battery Conditions

Use the internal voltage reference or a resistor divider to monitor supply voltage. If it drops below a threshold:

Alert the user (e.g., LED blink, warning signal)

Switch to ultra-low-power mode

Reduce sampling or transmission frequency

Disable non-essential features

Example using ADC to measure Vbat:

```
let vbat = adc.read(&vbat_channel).unwrap();

if vbat < VBAT_LOW_THRESHOLD {
    reduce_activity_mode(); // e.g., sample every
30 minutes instead
```

```
}
```

This keeps your application alive longer and avoids brownouts or corruption.

Avoid Flash and EEPROM Writes in Loops

Writing to flash or EEPROM consumes a lot of current, especially on older or cheaper parts. Avoid unnecessary write cycles.

Instead of logging every sample:

```
if significant_change_detected(new_value) {
    store_to_flash(new_value);
}
```

Also, **batch writes** when possible. Accumulate multiple readings in RAM and write them all at once to reduce energy cost per sample.

Don't Forget GPIO Pulls and Debug Pins

Debug interfaces like SWD, JTAG, or UART debug pins may keep the device from entering low-current states—especially if the debugger is connected.

In production:

Disable debug

Reconfigure debug pins as standard GPIO or analog inputs

Set all unused GPIOs to output-low or analog mode

This ensures the pins don't float or oscillate, which can waste current.

```
let _ = gpioa.pa13.into_analog(&mut gpioa.moder,
&mut gpioa.pupdr); // PA13 = SWDIO
```

Verify Behavior with Measurement

Once you structure your firmware properly, validate it by measuring:

Sleep current: should be single-digit microamps (for STOP/Standby)

Wake duration: milliseconds or less

Peripherals off when idle

138

Battery voltage tracking behavior

Use a current profiler, DMM + shunt resistor, or battery simulation tool to confirm that your firmware behaves the way you designed it to.

Writing battery-friendly applications is not about reducing clock speed alone—it's about designing your entire firmware lifecycle around **energy-conscious decisions**. In Rust, you get direct access to hardware, type safety, and the ability to structure tasks cleanly using async logic, RTIC tasks, or interrupt-driven scheduling.

Make wake events rare. Make processing fast. Keep peripherals off. Avoid redundant work. Measure everything. When you do these things, your firmware becomes more than functional—it becomes sustainable.

And that's the difference between a product that lasts three days and one that lasts three years on the same battery.

Chapter 8: Building Real-World Embedded Applications

Now that you've worked through the foundations—sleep modes, efficient peripheral usage, low-level register access, and battery optimization—it's time to bring it all together. Real-world embedded applications don't live in isolated code snippets. They are structured projects that read sensors, communicate data, manage timing, and evolve over time.

This chapter focuses on how to structure your code like a professional embedded developer, build and ship complete firmware with UART and wireless output, and prepare it for production and deployment. Along the way, you'll see how to manage assets, organize crates, and keep your embedded Rust applications scalable and maintainable.

Project Structure and Best Practices

The structure of your embedded Rust project is more than just how you organize files. It's the foundation of how you build, test, scale, and maintain your firmware. If your code is difficult to navigate, if every module depends on everything else, or if your build process is tangled and manual, you're setting yourself up for trouble as soon as the project grows or changes.

At the highest level, your embedded project should mirror the way you think about the application. Break it into logical pieces: hardware abstraction, device drivers, system state, and application logic. Each piece should be in its own module.

Here's a layout you'll often see in production-ready projects:

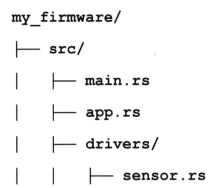

```
my_firmware/
├── src/
│   ├── main.rs
│   ├── app.rs
│   ├── drivers/
│   │   ├── sensor.rs
```

```
|   |   ├── uart.rs
|   |   ├── lora.rs
|   |   └── power.rs
|   ├── system/
|   |   ├── clock.rs
|   |   ├── sleep.rs
|   |   └── init.rs
|   ├── config.rs
|   └── types.rs
├── Cargo.toml
├── memory.x
└── .cargo/
    └── config.toml
```

Each module serves a single, focused purpose:

drivers/ handles hardware peripherals: sensor interfaces, UART, SPI radios, power rails.

system/ manages startup, clocks, and sleep behavior.

app.rs contains the application state machine or logic.

config.rs defines constants, thresholds, and tuning parameters.

types.rs defines shared structs and enums used across modules.

Avoid monolithic main.rs files with all logic in one place. Keep that file focused on top-level initialization and task orchestration.

Use Modules for Separation of Concerns

Rust's module system gives you clear namespace boundaries and private vs public visibility. Use this deliberately.

For example, your UART driver should only expose what the application needs:

```rust
// drivers/uart.rs
use embedded_hal::serial::Write;
use nb::block;

pub struct Logger<TX: Write<u8>> {
    tx: TX,
}

impl<TX: Write<u8>> Logger<TX> {
    pub fn new(tx: TX) -> Self {
        Self { tx }
    }

    pub fn log(&mut self, msg: &str) {
        for byte in msg.bytes() {
            block!(self.tx.write(byte)).ok();
        }
    }
}
```

Now in `main.rs` or `app.rs`, you just do:

```rust
let logger = Logger::new(tx);

logger.log("System initialized\n");
```

You don't leak the underlying HAL implementation or configuration logic into higher layers.

This kind of modularity helps when changing platforms or HALs—only the low-level driver changes, not the application.

Handle Initialization in One Place

All hardware setup—GPIOs, clocks, peripherals—should happen in a single place. Create an `init.rs` module to keep this logic clean.

```rust
// system/init.rs
pub struct Board {
    pub adc: Adc,
```

```
    pub tx: Tx<UART>,
    pub cs: OutputPin,
    // ...
}

pub fn init(dp: pac::Peripherals) -> Board {
    // setup clocks
    // configure GPIOs
    // initialize UART, SPI, ADC, etc.
}
```

Then in `main.rs`:

```
let board = init(dp);

let mut logger = Logger::new(board.tx);
logger.log("Startup complete\n");
```

You avoid repeating initialization logic across modules. It also makes the system easier to port—only `init.rs` needs to change for a new board variant.

Use `config.rs` for Tunables

Any constant that might need tuning or version-specific behavior should live in `config.rs`. This keeps your logic clean and makes adaptation easy.

```
// config.rs
pub const SENSOR_INTERVAL_SECS: u32 = 30;
pub const TEMP_THRESHOLD: u16 = 680;
pub const LORA_FREQ_MHZ: f32 = 868.1;
```

In your application logic:

```
if reading > config::TEMP_THRESHOLD {

    transmit_alert(reading);

}
```

This avoids scattering magic numbers throughout your codebase and helps in tuning without risky rewrites.

Define Custom Types in `types.rs`

When you find yourself reusing the same tuple or enum structure in multiple modules, define it explicitly in `types.rs`:

```
// types.rs
pub enum SensorEvent {
    Temperature(u16),
    Humidity(u16),
}

pub struct Packet {
    pub payload: [u8; 32],
    pub len: usize,
}
```

Now your modules stay focused, and shared types live in one central place.

Prefer RTIC for Task Scheduling

For projects with periodic sampling, event handling, or concurrent peripherals, `rtic` helps you maintain timing and safety. You get:

Interrupt-based task scheduling

Exclusive resource management

Clear separation between initialization, tasks, and idle behavior

Example `main.rs` using RTIC:

```
#[init]
fn init(ctx: init::Context) {
    // Hardware init
    schedule_sensor_task().unwrap();
}

#[task]
fn sensor_task(ctx: sensor_task::Context) {
    let value = read_sensor();
    log_value(value);
    sensor_task::spawn_after(30.secs()).unwrap();
}

#[idle]
fn idle(_: idle::Context) -> ! {
```

```
    loop {
        cortex_m::asm::wfi();
    }
}
```

You write tasks that are isolated and event-triggered. No polling loops. Minimal energy waste.

Version and Build Consistently

Use `Cargo.toml` metadata and embed version info in your firmware output:

```
writeln!(logger, "Firmware v{}\n",
env!("CARGO_PKG_VERSION")).ok();
```

Configure `.cargo/config.toml` for consistent builds:

```
[build]
target = "thumbv7em-none-eabihf"

[target.'thumbv7em-none-eabihf']
runner = "probe-rs run --chip STM32F303"
```

You can build and flash with:

```
cargo build --release

probe-rs flash --chip STM32F303 target/thumbv7em-
none-eabihf/release/my_firmware
```

This ensures consistency across environments.

Use Feature Flags for Platform Differences

If your project supports multiple hardware variants, define cargo features in `Cargo.toml`:

```
[features]

board_a = []

board_b = []

default = ["board_a"]
```

In your code:

```
#[cfg(feature = "board_a")]
pub fn configure_leds() {
    // Setup GPIOA
}

#[cfg(feature = "board_b")]
pub fn configure_leds() {
    // Setup GPIOB
}
```

Now your codebase can support multiple boards without duplicating logic.

Good structure doesn't just help you stay organized—it helps you debug, extend, refactor, and ship your code with confidence. A well-structured embedded Rust project makes it easy to:

Keep logic modular and testable

Swap hardware or drivers without rewriting application logic

Tune parameters cleanly

Manage growth as your firmware matures

Start small, keep responsibilities clear, and enforce boundaries between hardware access, logic, and configuration. By following these practices, you'll find your projects more reliable, maintainable, and portable—and you'll spend more time building features, not fixing fragile code.

Case Study: Sensor Logger with UART Output

Let's walk through a real-world embedded application: a sensor logger that periodically reads data from an analog temperature sensor and sends the result over UART to a host computer or serial terminal. This kind of system is useful in countless real environments—ranging from development boards used for experimentation to remote monitoring units that need to log or transmit sensor readings to an external controller.

The core goal here is to create an embedded firmware that wakes up on a schedule, samples the sensor quickly using the ADC peripheral, sends the data over a serial port, and then returns to a low-power state until the next interval. This project will demonstrate how to coordinate peripheral initialization, implement reliable logging, and manage power responsibly, using idiomatic and modular Rust.

System Overview

Here's what the application needs to do:

Initialize clocks, GPIOs, UART, and ADC.

Wake up every 30 seconds using a timer.

Read the temperature value via ADC.

Format and send that reading over UART.

Sleep until the next scheduled task.

We'll use the `stm32f3xx-hal` crate as an example HAL, and the `cortex-m-rtic` crate to structure tasks and interrupts cleanly.

Hardware Setup

You'll need:

A board like the STM32F303 Discovery or Nucleo.

A simple analog temperature sensor (like LM35 or TMP36) connected to an ADC-capable GPIO pin.

A USB-to-serial adapter (e.g., CP2102 or FTDI) connected to the TX pin for UART output.

A serial terminal on your host PC (like `screen`, `minicom`, or `PuTTY`).

Connect the analog sensor's output to a GPIO pin with ADC support—say, `PA0`.

Crate Dependencies

In **`Cargo.toml`**:

```toml
[dependencies]

cortex-m = "0.7"

cortex-m-rt = "0.7"

cortex-m-rtic = "1.1"

panic-halt = "0.2"

stm32f3xx-hal = { version = "0.8", features =
["stm32f303", "rt"] }

embedded-hal = "0.2"

nb = "1.0"
```

Make sure you also add a `memory.x` file and `.cargo/config.toml` to define the target and flash layout.

Main Application Code

Here's a full working example of the sensor logger, broken down and explained:

```rust
#![no_std]
#![no_main]

use cortex_m_rt::entry;
use panic_halt as _;
use rtic::app;
use stm32f3xx_hal::{
    adc::Adc,
    gpio::{gpioa::PA0, Analog},
    pac,
    prelude::*,
    serial::{Serial, Tx},
    timer::Timer,
};

use nb::block;
use core::fmt::Write;
```

```rust
#[app(device = stm32f3xx_hal::pac, peripherals =
true)]
mod app {
    use super::*;

    #[shared]
    struct Shared {}

    #[local]
    struct Local {
        adc: Adc<pac::ADC1>,
        pin: PA0<Analog>,
        tx: Tx<pac::USART1>,
        timer: Timer<pac::TIM2>,
    }

    #[init]
    fn init(ctx: init::Context) -> (Shared, Local,
init::Monotonics()) {
        let dp = ctx.device;

        let mut flash = dp.FLASH.constrain();
        let mut rcc = dp.RCC.constrain();
        let mut gpioa = dp.GPIOA.split(&mut
rcc.ahb);

        let clocks =
rcc.cfgr.sysclk(8.mhz()).freeze(&mut flash.acr);

        // UART: PA9 = TX, PA10 = RX (only TX used
here)
        let tx_pin = gpioa.pa9.into_af7(&mut
gpioa.moder, &mut gpioa.afrh);
        let rx_pin = gpioa.pa10.into_af7(&mut
gpioa.moder, &mut gpioa.afrh);
        let serial = Serial::usart1(dp.USART1,
(tx_pin, rx_pin), 9600.Bd(), clocks, &mut
rcc.apb2);
        let (tx, _) = serial.split();

        // ADC on PA0
```

```rust
        let analog_pin = gpioa.pa0.into_analog(&mut
gpioa.moder, &mut gpioa.pupdr);
        let mut adc = Adc::adc1(dp.ADC1, &mut
rcc.ahb, clocks);

adc.set_sample_time(stm32f3xx_hal::adc::SampleTime:
:T_71);

        // Timer for 30-second interval
        let mut timer = Timer::tim2(dp.TIM2,
1.hz(), clocks, &mut rcc.apb1);
        timer.start(30.secs());

        // Schedule first read
        sample::spawn().unwrap();

        (
            Shared {},
            Local {
                adc,
                pin: analog_pin,
                tx,
                timer,
            },
            init::Monotonics(),
        )
    }

    #[task(local = [adc, pin, tx, timer])]
    fn sample(ctx: sample::Context) {
        let raw =
ctx.local.adc.read(ctx.local.pin).unwrap();
        let millivolts = raw as u32 * 3300 / 4096;
        let temperature_celsius = millivolts / 10;
// For LM35: 10mV/°C

        let _ = writeln!(
            ctx.local.tx,
            "Temperature: {} °C (ADC raw: {})\r",
            temperature_celsius,
            raw
        );
```

```
            ctx.local.timer.start(30.secs());
            while ctx.local.timer.wait().is_err() {}

            sample::spawn().unwrap();
        }

        #[idle]
        fn idle(_: idle::Context) -> ! {
            loop {
                cortex_m::asm::wfi();
            }
        }
    }
```

Explanation

ADC Configuration: We use PA0 as an analog input to read the output voltage from the sensor. The sample time is increased to improve stability and accuracy.

UART Configuration: Only the TX pin is used here, so you can connect it to a USB serial adapter and see the output on your PC.

Timer: A 1Hz base timer is used and programmed to wait for 30 seconds. You could also use RTC for more accuracy and lower power consumption.

Logging: The sensor reading is formatted as a plain ASCII message and written to the UART using `writeln!`.

You can monitor the output in a terminal:

```
screen /dev/ttyUSB0 9600
```

You should see output like:

```
Temperature: 24 °C (ADC raw: 2980)
```

every 30 seconds.

Extending the Project

You can now extend this project by:

Logging values to flash memory (with a ring buffer).

Adding humidity or light sensors.

Replacing UART output with LoRa or BLE.

Writing the UART log to SD card via SPI.

Using RTC and STOP mode to reduce energy consumption.

These extensions will help you apply more advanced concepts from the rest of the book.

This sensor logger is a complete, usable embedded application. It shows how to tie ADC readings, UART output, and periodic timers into a clean, maintainable structure using Rust. With only a few modules and clear responsibilities, you can test, extend, and evolve this firmware for more complex tasks, while keeping your system responsive, efficient, and reliable. It's a solid foundation for building real embedded systems that are both powerful and battery-aware.

Case Study: Wireless Data Node Using LoRa or Bluetooth

When building real embedded systems that need to communicate beyond a single board, you often reach for wireless connectivity. Whether it's a soil moisture sensor reporting conditions from a farm field, or a wearable sending health data to a smartphone, the ability to transmit data wirelessly—efficiently and reliably—is crucial.

In this case study, we're going to build a practical wireless data node in embedded Rust. You'll learn how to collect sensor readings and send them wirelessly using two common options:

LoRa (Long Range Radio): Excellent for low-power, long-range communication in outdoor or industrial scenarios.

Bluetooth (BLE): Perfect for short-range, smartphone-compatible communication with low power usage.

We'll look at how to set up the hardware, write driver-compatible code, and structure the application so it can support either protocol with minimal changes.

Project Objective

This application:

Samples an analog temperature sensor every minute.

Formats the reading into a small packet.

Sends the packet wirelessly over LoRa or BLE.

Sleeps in STOP mode between transmissions to conserve battery.

This pattern fits many real-world use cases, from agricultural monitoring to personal tracking.

Hardware Setup Options

You can use one of two setups depending on the radio you have access to:

For LoRa:

Microcontroller (e.g., STM32F303, STM32L0x series).

Semtech SX1276/78 LoRa radio module.

SPI connection (SCK, MISO, MOSI, NSS).

Reset and optional DIO interrupt pins.

For BLE:

Microcontroller with UART interface.

BLE module (e.g., HM-10, RN4871, or nRF51822 module in HCI mode).

UART TX/RX connection.

Both options will require a sensor on an ADC pin and optionally a status LED.

Preparing the Project

Set up your project as discussed earlier:

```
cargo new --bin wireless_node

cd wireless_node
```
Configure your target in .cargo/config.toml:

```
[build]
target = "thumbv7em-none-eabihf"

[target.thumbv7em-none-eabihf]
runner = "probe-rs run --chip STM32F303"
```

And add dependencies to Cargo.toml:

```
[dependencies]

cortex-m = "0.7"

cortex-m-rt = "0.7"

cortex-m-rtic = "1.1"

panic-halt = "0.2"

embedded-hal = "0.2"

nb = "1.0"

stm32f3xx-hal = { version = "0.8", features =
["stm32f303", "rt"] }
```

If using an SX127x LoRa chip, you'll also need the radio-sx127x driver or a custom one based on embedded-hal.

Application Structure

Your project should include:

main.rs: The RTIC app entry point.

sensor.rs: ADC reading and sensor abstraction.

lora.rs or ble.rs: Radio interface logic.

sleep.rs: Power management routines.

Let's go through the key parts.

Sensor Module

```
// sensor.rs
use stm32f3xx_hal::adc::Adc;
use stm32f3xx_hal::gpio::{Analog, gpioa::PA0};

pub struct Sensor {
    pin: PA0<Analog>,
}

impl Sensor {
    pub fn new(pin: PA0<Analog>) -> Self {
        Sensor { pin }
    }

    pub fn read(&mut self, adc: &mut Adc) -> u16 {
        adc.read(&mut self.pin).unwrap()
    }
}
```

LoRa Communication Module

Here's a basic structure using an SPI-based LoRa driver.

```
// lora.rs
use embedded_hal::blocking::spi::Transfer;
use embedded_hal::digital::v2::OutputPin;
use radio_sx127x::{prelude::*, Sx127x};

pub struct LoRaRadio<SPI, CS, RESET> {
    driver: Sx127x<SPI, CS, RESET>,
}

impl<SPI, CS, RESET, E> LoRaRadio<SPI, CS, RESET>
where
    SPI: Transfer<u8, Error = E>,
    CS: OutputPin,
    RESET: OutputPin,
{
    pub fn new(spi: SPI, cs: CS, reset: RESET) ->
Self {
```

```rust
        let mut driver = Sx127x::new(spi, cs,
reset).unwrap();
        driver.set_frequency(868.0).unwrap();
        driver.set_tx_power(17).unwrap();
        Self { driver }
    }

    pub fn send(&mut self, data: &[u8]) {
        self.driver.transmit(data).unwrap();
    }
}
```

You'll need to initialize SPI, chip-select (CS), and reset pins in `init()`.

BLE Communication Module

If using a BLE module that accepts AT commands over UART:

```rust
// ble.rs
use embedded_hal::serial::Write;
use nb::block;

pub struct Ble<TX: Write<u8>> {
    tx: TX,
}

impl<TX: Write<u8>> Ble<TX> {
    pub fn new(tx: TX) -> Self {
        Self { tx }
    }

    pub fn send(&mut self, data: &str) {
        for b in data.bytes() {
            block!(self.tx.write(b)).ok();
        }
    }
}
```

You'd typically send something like:

```rust
ble.send("TEMP:24\r\n");
```

Modules like the HM-10 handle advertising and transmission internally.

156

Main Application Logic (RTIC)

```rust
#[app(device = stm32f3xx_hal::pac, peripherals =
true)]
mod app {
    use super::*;
    use cortex_m::asm;
    use stm32f3xx_hal::{
        prelude::*,
        adc::Adc,
        serial::{Serial, Tx},
        timer::Timer,
        gpio::{gpioa::PA0, Analog},
    };

    #[shared]
    struct Shared {}

    #[local]
    struct Local {
        adc: Adc<pac::ADC1>,
        sensor: Sensor,
        ble: Ble<Tx<pac::USART1>>, // or use
LoRaRadio if on LoRa
        timer: Timer<pac::TIM2>,
    }

    #[init]
    fn init(ctx: init::Context) -> (Shared, Local,
init::Monotonics()) {
        let dp = ctx.device;
        let mut flash = dp.FLASH.constrain();
        let mut rcc = dp.RCC.constrain();
        let mut gpioa = dp.GPIOA.split(&mut
rcc.ahb);
        let clocks = rcc.cfgr.freeze(&mut
flash.acr);

        let adc = Adc::adc1(dp.ADC1, &mut rcc.ahb,
clocks);
        let analog_pin = gpioa.pa0.into_analog(&mut
gpioa.moder, &mut gpioa.pupdr);
        let sensor = Sensor::new(analog_pin);
```

157

```
        // UART TX pin (PA9)
        let tx_pin = gpioa.pa9.into_af7(&mut
gpioa.moder, &mut gpioa.afrh);
        let rx_pin = gpioa.pa10.into_af7(&mut
gpioa.moder, &mut gpioa.afrh);
        let serial = Serial::usart1(dp.USART1,
(tx_pin, rx_pin), 9600.Bd(), clocks, &mut
rcc.apb2);
        let (tx, _) = serial.split();
        let ble = Ble::new(tx);

        let mut timer = Timer::tim2(dp.TIM2,
1.hz(), clocks, &mut rcc.apb1);
        timer.start(60.secs());

        transmit::spawn().unwrap();

        (Shared {}, Local { adc, sensor, ble, timer
}, init::Monotonics())
    }

    #[task(local = [sensor, adc, ble, timer])]
    fn transmit(ctx: transmit::Context) {
        let temp =
ctx.local.sensor.read(ctx.local.adc);
        let message = format!("TEMP:{}\r\n", temp);
        ctx.local.ble.send(&message);

        ctx.local.timer.start(60.secs());
        while ctx.local.timer.wait().is_err() {}

        transmit::spawn().unwrap();
    }

    #[idle]
    fn idle(_: idle::Context) -> ! {
        loop {
            asm::wfi(); // Enter sleep between
tasks
        }
    }
```

This application sends the temperature reading over BLE or LoRa every 60 seconds, sleeping in between to conserve energy.

Deployment Tips

If you're using LoRa, test with a gateway (e.g., TTN or LoRa-E5 dev board).

For BLE, connect via a BLE terminal app (e.g., LightBlue on iOS/Android).

Keep messages short to reduce radio-on time.

Use Stop or Standby mode when extending to battery power.

Consider ACKs and retries for LoRa reliability.

Wireless data nodes are at the center of most modern sensor networks. This case study shows how embedded Rust enables you to implement a clean, modular, and efficient wireless transmitter that's portable between different communication technologies. Whether you're targeting LoRa for long range or BLE for mobile integration, you can apply the same structure and principles to ensure your firmware is reliable, power-efficient, and easy to maintain.

Packaging and Releasing Firmware

Writing embedded firmware is only half the work—getting it reliably into the field, onto devices, and into the hands of other developers or stakeholders is the other half. Once your application is stable, structured, and tested, it needs to be packaged in a way that's reproducible, portable, and maintainable.

In embedded Rust, releasing firmware isn't just about flashing a `.bin` file to one board—it's about preparing versioned builds, defining memory layouts, maintaining hardware compatibility, and optionally automating deployment using CI tools. This section walks you through everything involved in taking your embedded Rust firmware from your development environment to a tagged, sharable, and flashable release.

Define a Target and Memory Layout

Every embedded firmware project must define:

The architecture and CPU target triple

The memory layout (FLASH and RAM)

The reset vector and interrupt table

This is done through a combination of a .cargo/config.toml file and a memory.x linker script.

.cargo/config.toml:

```
[build]
target = "thumbv7em-none-eabihf"

[target.thumbv7em-none-eabihf]
runner = "probe-rs run --chip STM32F303"
```

This tells cargo to always build for the Cortex-M4F target and use probe-rs to flash and run your firmware.

memory.x:

```
MEMORY

{

  FLASH : ORIGIN = 0x08000000, LENGTH = 256K

  RAM   : ORIGIN = 0x20000000, LENGTH = 40K

}
```

This tells the linker where your program will reside in flash and where RAM begins. These values depend on the specific microcontroller you're using. Always check the datasheet or the chip's reference manual.

Then, in main.rs, make sure to link the memory script:

```
#![no_std]
#![no_main]

use cortex_m_rt::entry;
```

The #[entry] attribute from cortex-m-rt uses the memory layout to place the reset vector correctly.

Enable Optimized Release Builds

By default, `cargo build` produces a debug binary with no optimizations. For embedded work, you want to use `--release` to enable compiler optimizations that reduce binary size and improve performance.

```
cargo build --release
```

To customize optimizations for embedded targets, edit your `Cargo.toml`:

```
[profile.release]

codegen-units = 1

lto = true

debug = true

opt-level = "z"
```

This configuration:

Enables link-time optimization (LTO)

Reduces code size (`opt-level = "z"`)

Keeps debug symbols for inspection (optional)

Build Artifacts

After building, your binary is located at:

```
target/thumbv7em-none-
eabihf/release/your_project_name
```

You can convert this ELF file to `.bin` or `.hex` format using `objcopy`:

```
arm-none-eabi-objcopy -O binary
target/.../your_project_name your_project.bin
```

Or use `cargo-binutils` to simplify this:

```
cargo install cargo-binutils
rustup component add llvm-tools-preview
```

```
cargo objcopy --release -- -O binary firmware.bin
```

Flash to Hardware

The most common tools for flashing Rust firmware to embedded boards are:

1. probe-rs

Probe-rs works with J-Link, ST-Link, CMSIS-DAP, and others.

```
cargo install probe-rs-cli

probe-rs download --chip STM32F303 firmware.bin
```

Or integrate it directly in `.cargo/config.toml` for `cargo run`:

```
[target.thumbv7em-none-eabihf]

runner = "probe-rs run --chip STM32F303"
```

Now you can simply run:

```
cargo run --release
```

2. dfu-util (for USB DFU Bootloaders)

If your board supports DFU, use:

```
dfu-util -a 0 -s 0x08000000:leave -D firmware.bin
```

3. STM32CubeProgrammer / OpenOCD

Useful for ST-Link and more manual workflows. Configure `.cfg` files appropriately.

Versioning Your Firmware

Always embed version info in your firmware binary. This helps when debugging, updating, or releasing patches.

In `Cargo.toml`:

```
[package]

name = "sensor_node"
```

162

```
version = "1.2.3"
```

In your code:

```
let _ = writeln!(uart, "Firmware v{}",
env!("CARGO_PKG_VERSION"));
```

This pulls in the version number at compile time and includes it in the UART output, a BLE broadcast, or your LoRa packet.

You can also include build timestamps and Git commit hashes using environment variables:

```
[build-dependencies]

vergen = "8"
```

Then in `build.rs`:

```
fn main() {
    vergen::EmitBuilder::new()
        .build_timestamp()
        .git_sha(true)
        .emit()
        .unwrap();
}
```

And in your code:

```
let _ = writeln!(uart, "Built at: {}",
env!("VERGEN_BUILD_TIMESTAMP"));
```

Release with Git Tags

Use Git tags to mark official firmware versions:

```
git tag v1.2.3

git push origin v1.2.3
```

This lets your team or automation pipelines grab specific builds. You can even attach binaries to GitHub releases for download and OTA distribution.

Optional: Automating Releases with Justfiles

A `justfile` is like a Makefile but easier to read. Here's an example:

```
build:

    cargo build --release


bin:

    cargo objcopy --release -- -O binary
firmware.bin


flash:

    probe-rs download --chip STM32F303 firmware.bin


release: build bin flash
```

Then you can simply run:

```
just release
```

For consistent packaging and flashing.

Checklist for a Shippable Firmware

Before you release:

All debug logging stripped or switched to release-level output

Power modes tested and active

Sleep logic confirmed and measured

Version string embedded and visible

Boot tested from power-on, not just after flashing

Panic behavior defined (e.g., reset, UART message, LED blink)

Releasing embedded Rust firmware professionally means more than compiling code—it means wrapping your build, versioning, flashing, and packaging into a repeatable, clear, and trackable process. With memory layout definitions, optimized builds, embedded version info, and structured release commands, your firmware becomes reliable—not just when it runs, but when it gets handed off to others.

This release workflow also sets the stage for long-term maintainability—whether you're pushing updates in the field, managing multiple hardware variants, or supporting products across multiple versions. Your firmware is now not just working code, but a reliable, deliverable product.

Chapter 9: Debugging, Testing, and Maintenance

As your embedded projects grow from blinking LEDs to full-featured, battery-efficient, wireless sensor nodes, you'll eventually face issues that aren't obvious. Unexpected resets, peripheral misbehavior, sleep modes that never wake up, and hard faults that crash your system silently—these are all normal challenges in embedded development.

To deal with them effectively, you need structured debugging tools, reliable testing strategies, and a clear plan for ongoing maintenance. Embedded Rust gives you the ability to write safe and expressive firmware, but you still need the right habits and tools to trace bugs, simulate conditions, and keep your codebase healthy over time.

Logging with defmt and RTT

In embedded systems, logging isn't just useful—it's essential. When your firmware fails silently or behaves inconsistently, and you don't have access to a screen, file system, or even a UART pin, logging becomes your window into the device's internal state. But logging has a cost, especially in resource-constrained environments. You can't afford to flood serial buffers, slow down execution, or consume unnecessary power.

This is where `defmt`—a compact, structured logging framework designed for embedded Rust—paired with **Real-Time Transfer (RTT)**, becomes one of your most valuable tools.

With `defmt`, you can log data with low runtime overhead and zero allocations. And with RTT, you can stream logs over your debugger interface (such as SWD) without needing a UART port. This lets you debug even in production-style builds, where serial output isn't available or desirable.

`defmt` stands for **deferred formatting**. Instead of formatting your log strings on the device, which is expensive in terms of memory and CPU cycles, it sends compact, encoded messages over RTT and decodes them on the host. This reduces the amount of data transmitted and avoids runtime formatting altogether.

166

Here's what that means in practice:

```
defmt::info!("Temperature: {}", 24);
```

On the device: this emits a binary blob using a compact index.

On your host machine: the logging tool knows what that index means and renders it as:

```
INFO  Temperature: 24
```

This keeps your firmware lean and fast, while giving you rich diagnostics during development.

Setting Up defmt in Your Project

To use `defmt` and RTT, you need to make a few adjustments to your project:

1. Add dependencies in `Cargo.toml`:

```
[dependencies]

defmt = "0.3"

defmt-rtt = "0.4"

panic-probe = { version = "0.3", features =
["print-defmt"] }


[dependencies.stm32f3xx-hal]

version = "0.8"
features = ["rt", "stm32f303", "defmt"]
```

You're telling the HAL to use `defmt` instead of the default `log`-based logging. `panic-probe` ensures that panics are also printed through the `defmt` interface.

2. Update `main.rs` or your entry point:

```
#![no_std]
#![no_main]

use panic_probe as _;
```

```rust
use defmt_rtt as _;
use defmt::*;
use cortex_m_rt::entry;

#[entry]
fn main() -> ! {
    info!("Starting firmware...");
    loop {
        debug!("Heartbeat");
        cortex_m::asm::delay(8_000_000); // Wait
~1s at 8 MHz
    }
}
```

Once this compiles, you're ready to connect and read the logs.

Running and Viewing Logs

1. Install `probe-rs` and `defmt-print`:

```
cargo install probe-rs-cli
```

```
cargo install defmt-print
```

2. Build the firmware:

```
cargo build --release
```

Make sure you're using the correct target in `.cargo/config.toml`:

```
[build]
```

```
target = "thumbv7em-none-eabihf"
```

3. Run and stream logs:

```
cargo run --release
```

This will flash the firmware and open a live log window like:

```
INFO  Starting firmware...
```

```
DEBUG Heartbeat
```

168

```
DEBUG Heartbeat

DEBUG Heartbeat
```
You'll see the logs as they're emitted over RTT, without needing UART or additional peripherals.

Using Log Levels and Tags

defmt supports multiple levels of verbosity:

```
defmt::trace!("Extremely detailed logs");

defmt::debug!("Useful for development");

defmt::info!("Informative message");

defmt::warn!("Something unusual happened");

defmt::error!("Something is wrong");
```

You can filter log levels during runtime by configuring the defmt tool, or compile-time by changing your build settings.

You can also include additional context in structured logs:

```
let temp = 27;

let battery = 3.72;

info!("Readings -> temp: {}, battery: {}", temp,
battery);
```

The output will be consistent, timestamped (if you enable timestamps), and easy to parse.

Logging in RTIC Applications

If you're using RTIC, logging works exactly the same inside your tasks:

```
#[task]
fn sample_sensor(ctx: sample_sensor::Context) {
    let temp = read_temp();
    info!("Temp reading: {}", temp);
}
```

You can even log from interrupts, just be careful with high-frequency events to avoid overwhelming RTT.

What If Logging Stops Working?

If you're not seeing logs:

Ensure the RTT buffer isn't overflowing.

Make sure you've flashed the `.elf` file that contains defmt symbols.

Check your debug probe—only SWD-capable debuggers can carry RTT.

Try `cargo embed` if you're using the `probe-rs` ecosystem and want an all-in-one tool.

Also make sure you're not using conflicting panic handlers like `panic-halt` or `panic-abort`. Only use one: `panic-probe`.

Logging in Production: Should You Leave It In?

This depends.

If your device will be deployed in difficult-to-debug environments (field sensors, industrial controllers), it's a great idea to:

Keep minimal `defmt::info!` or `defmt::error!` logs enabled.

Use debug headers or pinouts that expose SWD so you can attach and inspect later.

Avoid UART logging unless necessary—it costs power and I/O.

Because `defmt` is compiled out when unused, leaving `debug!` or `trace!` calls in your code doesn't cost anything if you compile without them.

`defmt` with RTT is the most efficient, developer-friendly logging solution available for embedded Rust. It offers:

Fast, compact runtime behavior.

Structured, formatted logs decoded on the host.

A low-power alternative to UART-based printing.

Seamless integration with the `probe-rs` toolchain.

Use it in every project. Build your logging habits early. It will save you hours of trial-and-error debugging, especially when you're troubleshooting power behavior, state machines, or initialization bugs. In the next section, you'll learn how to combine this logging with mock-based testing to verify your logic even without running on real hardware.

Testing Embedded Code with Mocks

In embedded development, testing is notoriously difficult to get right. You typically don't have the luxury of full-featured operating systems, dynamic memory allocation, or even a console to print test output. Worse, your code usually interacts directly with hardware—ADC readings, I2C sensors, GPIO pins, and timers—which makes it hard to isolate logic from real peripherals. But just because your code runs on a microcontroller doesn't mean it should be untested.

With Rust, and especially its trait system, you have a clear path to building testable firmware—even before your hardware is ready. You can write and run tests on your laptop, simulate sensor behavior, assert correctness of outputs, and gain real confidence in your code. All of this is made possible through **mocking**—replacing hardware-dependent code with software implementations that act the same but work in any environment.

Why Use Mocks?

Mocks let you replace hardware components (like an I2C sensor or a GPIO pin) with simulated versions that:

Return known values for repeatable testing

Track what your code is doing

Help you assert that logic is functioning correctly

This is critical when:

You want to test logic without a dev board

You're debugging edge cases like low battery or faulty sensor data

You're developing higher-level firmware before your PCB is manufactured

You're working in CI where hardware isn't available

Designing for Testability: Use Traits

Let's say you have a temperature logger that samples a sensor and triggers a warning if the reading is too high.

Start by defining the behavior in a trait:

```
pub trait TemperatureSensor {

    fn read_celsius(&mut self) -> u16;

}
```

Now your main logic uses this trait, not a specific sensor driver:

```
pub struct Monitor<S: TemperatureSensor> {
    sensor: S,
    threshold: u16,
}

impl<S: TemperatureSensor> Monitor<S> {
    pub fn new(sensor: S, threshold: u16) -> Self {
        Self { sensor, threshold }
    }

    pub fn check(&mut self) -> Option<String> {
        let temp = self.sensor.read_celsius();
        if temp > self.threshold {
            Some(format!("High temp: {}°C", temp))
        } else {
            None
        }
    }
}
```

This logic doesn't depend on the actual sensor—it only relies on the behavior defined in the trait. Now you can plug in a mock sensor for testing.

Writing a Simple Mock for Unit Testing

In your `tests/` folder or as a `#[cfg(test)]` module in the same file:

```rust
#[cfg(test)]
mod tests {
    use super::*;

    struct FakeSensor {
        value: u16,
    }

    impl TemperatureSensor for FakeSensor {
        fn read_celsius(&mut self) -> u16 {
            self.value
        }
    }

    #[test]
    fn triggers_warning_if_temperature_is_high() {
        let sensor = FakeSensor { value: 75 };
        let mut monitor = Monitor::new(sensor, 70);

        let result = monitor.check();
        assert_eq!(result, Some("High temp:
75°C".to_string()));
    }

    #[test]
    fn does_nothing_when_temperature_is_safe() {
        let sensor = FakeSensor { value: 60 };
        let mut monitor = Monitor::new(sensor, 70);

        let result = monitor.check();
        assert_eq!(result, None);
    }
}
```

You're now running embedded logic tests using the standard `cargo test` command on your host system:

```
cargo test
```

No dev board needed. You can test multiple edge cases in seconds.

Testing Hardware Abstractions with `embedded-hal-mock`

Rust's `embedded-hal` defines traits for common peripherals—digital I/O, SPI, I2C, etc.—and there's a dedicated mock crate that lets you simulate those in tests.

Add it to your dev dependencies:

```
[dev-dependencies]

embedded-hal-mock = "0.9"
```

Example: testing an I2C sensor driver.

Suppose you have a driver like:

```
pub struct TempSensor<I2C> {
    i2c: I2C,
    address: u8,
}

impl<I2C, E> TempSensor<I2C>
where
    I2C:
embedded_hal::blocking::i2c::WriteRead<Error = E>,
{
    pub fn new(i2c: I2C, address: u8) -> Self {
        Self { i2c, address }
    }

    pub fn read(&mut self) -> Result<u16, E> {
        let mut buf = [0; 2];
        self.i2c.write_read(self.address, &[0x00],
&mut buf)?;
        Ok(u16::from_be_bytes(buf))
    }
}
```

Now test it:

```
#[cfg(test)]
mod tests {
    use super::*;
```

```
    use embedded_hal_mock::i2c::{Mock as I2cMock,
Transaction as I2cTransaction};

    #[test]
    fn reads_temperature_from_sensor() {
        let expectations = [
            I2cTransaction::write_read(0x48,
vec![0x00], vec![0x01, 0x90]),
        ];
        let mock = I2cMock::new(&expectations);

        let mut sensor = TempSensor::new(mock,
0x48);
        let value = sensor.read().unwrap();

        assert_eq!(value, 400);
        sensor.i2c.done(); // ensure all
transactions were used
    }
}
```

You simulate an I2C device responding with `[0x01, 0x90]`, which is `400` in big-endian. The mock validates that the correct commands were sent, and your test confirms correct interpretation.

Testing Time-Based Behavior

Sometimes you want to simulate timers or sleep-based behavior. One way is to model time passage with a fake timer.

```
pub trait Timer {
    fn elapsed_ms(&self) -> u32;
}

struct MockTimer(u32);

impl Timer for MockTimer {
    fn elapsed_ms(&self) -> u32 {
        self.0
    }
}
```

Use the timer in your logic and assert that behavior changes based on time. This lets you write tests for watchdogs, timeouts, backoffs, etc.

What You Can Test Without Hardware

With this approach, you can test:

Sensor reading and conversion logic

Threshold detection

Peripheral command sequences (I2C, SPI)

State machines and transitions

Timer and debounce logic

Command encoding and protocol parsers

And all of this runs on your dev machine with no need to flash firmware.

Best Practices for Testable Embedded Code

Use traits for all hardware interactions

Avoid hardcoding peripherals inside logic

Write modules that take dependencies as generic parameters

Avoid `static mut` unless absolutely needed

Isolate business logic from device setup

Put your core logic in libraries, not only in `main.rs`

These patterns let you reuse the same code across hardware and tests, and they keep your firmware modular and reliable.

Testing embedded firmware is not just possible—it's practical and powerful with Rust. By leaning into traits, modular structure, and mock implementations, you can develop robust systems with confidence, even before a single byte is flashed to hardware.

With the help of `embedded-hal-mock` and standard test tools, you can simulate hardware behavior, assert correct operation, and prevent regressions.

Combined with logging and CI, this gives you a serious edge as your projects grow in complexity and scope.

Flashing, Debugging, and GDB Integration

At some point in every embedded project, something breaks and you can't tell why. It could be an unexpected hard fault, a timer that never fires, or a peripheral that silently stops responding. Logging is useful—but sometimes it's not enough. You need to stop the CPU, inspect registers, step through code, and analyze what's happening in real time. That's where proper **flashing and debugging** with tools like **GDB** and **probe-rs** becomes essential.

Rust's embedded ecosystem supports first-class debugging with modern open-source tools. You can flash your firmware to a board, halt execution, step through your source code, inspect variables, and even monitor memory live while your program runs.

Preparing for Flashing and Debugging

Before you can flash or debug, you need:

A supported debug probe (e.g., ST-Link, J-Link, CMSIS-DAP).

A microcontroller that exposes SWD or JTAG pins.

A properly built .elf file with debug symbols.

Your target microcontroller correctly defined in probe-rs.

Let's walk through how to configure and use all of this.

Building the Firmware for Debugging

Always build your firmware in **release mode**, but with **debug symbols** preserved.

In Cargo.toml:

```
[profile.release]

opt-level = "z"

debug = true
```

```
lto = true

codegen-units = 1
```

Then build with:

```
cargo build --release
```

This produces an optimized `.elf` file with symbol info needed for debugging. The file will be in:

```
target/thumbv7em-none-eabihf/release/your_project
```

This ELF file contains the binary, symbol table, and section layout—all critical for GDB.

Installing Required Tools

You'll need:

probe-rs CLI

`gdb` (from ARM toolchain)

Install **probe-rs:**

```
cargo install probe-rs-cli
```

Install ARM GDB (via system package manager or ARM toolchain):

```
# Ubuntu/Debian
sudo apt install gdb-multiarch

# macOS (with ARM toolchain)
brew install arm-none-eabi-gcc
```

Flashing Firmware with probe-rs

To flash your firmware:

```
probe-rs download --chip STM32F303 firmware.elf
```

This writes your `.elf` file to the microcontroller's flash, performs a reset, and halts or runs depending on settings.

178

You can also specify custom configuration using a `.yaml` file or select the probe if multiple devices are connected.

Using GDB to Debug Firmware

Step 1: Start the GDB Stub

Launch the GDB server interface provided by probe-rs:

```
probe-rs gdb --chip STM32F303
```

This opens a GDB remote stub at TCP port 1337.

You'll see:

```
Waiting for GDB connection on port 1337
```

Step 2: Launch GDB and Connect

In another terminal:

```
arm-none-eabi-gdb target/thumbv7em-none-
eabihf/release/your_project
```

Inside GDB:

```
(gdb) target remote :1337

(gdb) load

(gdb) monitor reset

(gdb) break main

(gdb) continue
```

You can now interactively control execution.

Common GDB Commands

```
break <function or file:line>    # Set a breakpoint

continue                         # Run the program

next                             # Step over

step                             # Step into
```

```
finish                          # Finish current function

print <var>                     # Print variable value

x/<format> <addr>               # Examine memory

info registers                  # Show CPU register values
```

For example:

```
(gdb) break sample::run

(gdb) continue

(gdb) print temp_reading

(gdb) x/4xb &sensor_buffer
```

This allows you to halt at a specific task, inspect variables, and verify if logic is executing as expected.

Debugging Hard Faults

If your firmware enters a hard fault, GDB can show you the cause:

```
(gdb) info registers

(gdb) backtrace
```

Or decode the faulting instruction address:

```
(gdb) x/i $pc
```

You can also set a watchpoint to monitor memory changes:

```
(gdb) watch *0x20000000
```

This is useful for debugging unexpected writes to variables or memory corruption.

Integrating probe-run for Flash + Run + Debug

If you prefer a simpler workflow, use `probe-run`:

```
cargo install probe-run
```
Then run:

```
cargo run --release
```

```
probe-run:
```
Builds your firmware

Flashes it

Displays `defmt` logs

Halts on panics

Provides backtraces when things go wrong

This is a more ergonomic alternative to raw GDB for many workflows.

Using `cargo-embed` for RTT + Flash + Logging

`cargo-embed` is another all-in-one tool built on probe-rs:

```
cargo install cargo-embed
```

Create an `Embed.toml`:

```
chip = "STM32F303"

log_enabled = true
```

Then run:

```
cargo embed --release
```

This handles flashing and RTT logging via defmt in one command. It's excellent for development workflows that involve frequent re-flashing and inspecting live logs.

Troubleshooting Flash and Debug

If things aren't working:

Confirm your chip is supported with `probe-rs list-chips`.

Try specifying the chip explicitly in commands.

Make sure SWD/JTAG is connected correctly.

Use `probe-rs info` to verify the probe can connect.

181

If using ST-Link, update its firmware via STM32CubeProgrammer.

Also check that your `.elf` file matches your target architecture (`thumbv7em-none-eabihf` for STM32F3).

Flashing and debugging are essential parts of embedded development, and Rust gives you professional-grade tools to do it right. With `probe-rs`, GDB, and `cargo-embed`, you can:

Inspect your firmware in real time

Catch subtle logic bugs

Analyze crashes with backtraces

Monitor memory and I/O directly

Integrate flashing and debugging into your workflow with minimal effort

When combined with structured logging (`defmt`) and unit testing (with mocks), this setup gives you full observability and control over your embedded system—without relying on guesswork or trial and error. In the next section, we'll explore how to automate these steps in CI pipelines so your firmware builds, tests, and flashes reliably every time.

Setting Up Continuous Integration for Embedded Projects

When you're building embedded firmware, it's easy to focus only on the hardware and ignore the long-term quality and reproducibility of your code. But the truth is, even microcontroller code benefits immensely from Continuous Integration (CI). A good CI setup automatically builds your project, runs tests, checks formatting, and catches breaking changes before they ever land on a production board.

Embedded Rust makes this even more powerful because your firmware is written in a modern, safe systems language that plays well with automated tooling. Whether you're testing sensor logic with mocks, compiling for multiple targets, or ensuring your builds don't regress, setting up CI will save you hours of manual work and give you confidence in every change you make.

Why CI Matters in Embedded Work

Without CI, here's what typically happens:

You make a change.

You build locally (maybe in release mode, maybe not).

You flash it to one board.

It works—so you merge the change.

This might seem fine—until a teammate pulls your code and can't build it. Or until you push a regression that only shows up in release mode. Or you break a mocked test that was never run because it wasn't in your build process.

CI solves this by enforcing a repeatable, testable, version-controlled build process. Every commit is verified against a known toolchain and target before it's accepted.

Basic CI Pipeline Overview

Let's define what you want your embedded CI pipeline to do:

Build the firmware for your target architecture (`thumbv7em-none-eabihf`).

Run unit tests using mocked components on the host.

Check formatting and code hygiene (`rustfmt`, `clippy`).

Optionally produce flashable binaries as artifacts.

Enforce this check on every commit or pull request.

You'll do all of this using GitHub Actions.

Set Up GitHub Actions

In your project root, create the file `.github/workflows/ci.yml`:

```
name: Embedded Rust CI

on:
  push:
    branches: [main]
  pull_request:
    branches: [main]
```

```
jobs:
  build:
    name: Build & Test
    runs-on: ubuntu-latest

    steps:
    - name: Checkout code
      uses: actions/checkout@v4

    - name: Install Rust and target
      uses: actions-rs/toolchain@v1
      with:
        toolchain: stable
        override: true
        target: thumbv7em-none-eabihf

    - name: Install Cargo utilities
      run: |
        cargo install cargo-binutils
        rustup component add llvm-tools-preview

    - name: Build release firmware
      run: cargo build --release --target
thumbv7em-none-eabihf

    - name: Run host-side tests
      run: cargo test

    - name: Check formatting
      run: cargo fmt --check

    - name: Lint for warnings
      run: cargo clippy -- -D warnings

    - name: Extract binary artifacts
      run: |
        mkdir -p output
        cargo objcopy --release --target thumbv7em-
none-eabihf -- -O binary output/firmware.bin
        cargo objcopy --release --target thumbv7em-
none-eabihf -- -O ihex output/firmware.hex
```

```
- name: Upload artifacts
  uses: actions/upload-artifact@v3
  with:
    name: firmware
    path: output/
```

This workflow does the following:

Checks out your project from GitHub.

Installs Rust and your embedded target (`thumbv7em-none-eabihf` for Cortex-M4).

Builds the firmware in release mode.

Runs any unit tests written for the host.

Validates formatting with `cargo fmt`.

Enforces warning-free builds with `clippy`.

Extracts `.bin` and `.hex` images.

Uploads those images as downloadable artifacts.

Simulating Embedded Tests on Host

You can't run full firmware on the CI server, but you can test business logic using mocks.

Here's an example test:

```
#[cfg(test)]
mod tests {
    use super::*;

    struct FakeSensor;

    impl Sensor for FakeSensor {
        fn read(&mut self) -> u16 {
            350
        }
    }
}
```

```
#[test]
fn triggers_alarm_when_temperature_is_high() {
    let mut system = Monitor::new(FakeSensor,
300);
    let result = system.check();
    assert!(result.is_some());
}
}
```

These tests run with `cargo test`, no hardware needed. In CI, this confirms your logic is sound.

Ensuring Firmware Artifacts are Usable

After CI builds your `.elf` file, you use `cargo objcopy` to create flashable formats:

```
cargo objcopy --release --target thumbv7em-none-
eabihf -- -O binary firmware.bin
```

These files are automatically attached to your GitHub build as artifacts, so you or your team can download them and flash directly using `probe-rs`:

```
probe-rs download --chip STM32F303 firmware.bin
```

This is especially helpful when you're preparing pre-release firmware or want to share test builds with other developers or QA engineers.

Expanding to Hardware-in-the-Loop (Optional)

Later, when you're ready to test on real hardware, you can:

Use a Raspberry Pi or CI runner with physical access to a dev board.

Flash the firmware using `probe-rs` CLI tools.

Read back telemetry via USB or UART.

Use hardware signals to verify correct behavior (e.g., LEDs or GPIO pulses).

Log results and pass/fail the job accordingly.

This brings real-world confidence into your automated tests. It's more complex, but also incredibly powerful for release validation.

186

Tips for Successful Embedded CI

Keep tests fast: CI should complete in under 3–5 minutes if possible.

Separate logic from hardware early using traits and mockable drivers.

Add version output to your firmware (e.g., with `env!("CARGO_PKG_VERSION")`).

Use Git tags (`v1.0.0`) to trigger releases and attach built binaries.

Store firmware release metadata alongside `.bin` or `.hex` files.

Continuous Integration isn't just for web apps—it's a vital part of embedded systems too. With Rust, you can write firmware that's not only safe and efficient, but also testable, buildable, and verifiable at every stage of development.

By integrating GitHub Actions into your embedded Rust workflow, you gain:

Confidence that your code builds consistently

Early detection of breakage across refactors

A foundation for hardware-in-the-loop testing later

Easy sharing of reproducible, flashable firmware builds

CI becomes your automated engineering assistant—watching every commit, running your tests, checking your formatting, and preparing your firmware for real-world use. Whether you're building a hobby project or commercial-grade product, this setup will serve you well.

Chapter 10: Future Directions and Advanced Topics

Once you've mastered the essentials of embedded Rust—memory-safe firmware, hardware abstraction, real-time behavior, peripheral integration, and production deployment—you start to look at what comes next. How can you make your firmware more efficient, more modular, more responsive? What options do you have for field updates without physical access? What if you want to explore other architectures beyond ARM? And if embedded Rust has helped you build something solid, how can you give back to the ecosystem?

This final chapter explores exactly that. We'll walk through some of the advanced and forward-looking capabilities emerging in the embedded Rust space: async firmware using **Embassy**, adding support for **OTA updates**, expanding to **RISC-V and other architectures**, and getting involved in **community contributions** that push the entire ecosystem forward.

Async Embedded Programming with Embassy

When you're building embedded systems with multiple tasks—like blinking LEDs, reading sensors, handling user input, or communicating over UART or I2C—you're often faced with a common challenge: concurrency. Traditionally, embedded developers rely on interrupt handlers, blocking APIs, polling loops, or cooperative schedulers to manage timing and responsiveness. But with Rust's powerful async/await syntax and the **Embassy** framework, you get a modern, safe, and highly efficient alternative for writing concurrent embedded applications.

Embassy brings structured async programming to embedded systems by providing a low-footprint executor, safe peripheral drivers, and time-based abstractions that run on bare-metal without a traditional RTOS. It allows you to write expressive code that behaves predictably and performs well, even on resource-constrained microcontrollers.

Embedded development typically involves waiting—for input from sensors, for timeouts to expire, for peripheral responses. If you write synchronous code, these waits are often handled by busy loops or timers that block execution, which:

Wastes CPU cycles and power

Makes it harder to run multiple tasks concurrently

Introduces complexity when coordinating multiple interrupts or peripheral events

With `async` programming, you avoid blocking. When your code waits, the executor suspends that task and allows others to run. In Rust, this is done with **zero-cost futures**—there's no dynamic allocation or hidden scheduling costs. Embassy builds on this to provide an async runtime for `no_std`, bare-metal applications.

Installing Embassy

Let's walk through how to set up Embassy in an embedded Rust project targeting STM32F3. Embassy supports several MCUs via feature flags, including STM32, nRF, RP2040, and ESP chips.

1. Set your target:

In `.cargo/config.toml`:

```
[build]

target = "thumbv7em-none-eabihf"
```

2. Add Embassy and HAL dependencies:

```
[dependencies]
embassy-stm32 = { version = "0.1", features =
["stm32f303", "defmt", "time-driver-any"] }
embassy-executor = { version = "0.3", features =
["integrated-timers"] }
embassy-time = "0.1"
embassy-sync = "0.3"
defmt = "0.3"
defmt-rtt = "0.4"
panic-probe = { version = "0.3", features =
["print-defmt"] }
```

189

```
cortex-m-rt = "0.7"
```

Writing Your First Async Firmware

Let's write a simple async task that blinks an LED every second.

```
#![no_std]
#![no_main]

use defmt_rtt as _;
use panic_probe as _;

use embassy_executor::Spawner;
use embassy_stm32::Peripherals;
use embassy_stm32::gpio::{Level, Output, Speed,
Pin};
use embassy_stm32::Config;
use embassy_time::{Duration, Timer};

#[embassy_executor::main]
async fn main(_spawner: Spawner, p: Peripherals) {
    let mut led = Output::new(p.PA5, Level::Low,
Speed::Low);

    loop {
        led.set_high();

Timer::after(Duration::from_millis(500)).await;

        led.set_low();

Timer::after(Duration::from_millis(500)).await;
    }
}
```

This example:

Configures PA5 as an output (commonly the LED pin on many boards)

Uses Timer::after().await to yield to the executor without blocking

Blinks the LED on and off every 500ms, in a fully async loop

No polling, no blocking, and no RTOS required.

Running Multiple Tasks Concurrently

The true strength of Embassy is its ability to manage multiple tasks efficiently. You can define and spawn concurrent tasks using the `Spawner`.

```rust
#[embassy_executor::task]
async fn blink(mut led: Output<'static, impl Pin>)
{
    loop {
        led.set_high();
        Timer::after(Duration::from_secs(1)).await;
        led.set_low();
        Timer::after(Duration::from_secs(1)).await;
    }
}

#[embassy_executor::task]
async fn status_loop() {
    loop {
        defmt::info!("Running status check...");
        Timer::after(Duration::from_secs(3)).await;
    }
}

#[embassy_executor::main]
async fn main(spawner: Spawner, p: Peripherals) {
    let led = Output::new(p.PA5, Level::Low,
Speed::Low);

    spawner.spawn(blink(led)).unwrap();
    spawner.spawn(status_loop()).unwrap();

    // main() continues running if needed
}
```

Each task is scheduled cooperatively by Embassy. When a task hits an `.await`, it yields to the executor, allowing others to run. This model is extremely memory efficient and power-friendly on microcontrollers.

Handling Peripherals Asynchronously

Embassy includes async drivers for peripherals such as UART, SPI, I2C, and more.

Here's an example of sending and receiving UART data asynchronously:

```
use embassy_stm32::usart::{Uart, Config as
UartConfig};

#[embassy_executor::task]
async fn echo_task(mut uart: Uart<'static, impl
embassy_stm32::usart::Instance>) {
    let mut buf = [0u8; 32];
    loop {
        let n = uart.read(&mut buf).await.unwrap();
        uart.write(&buf[..n]).await.unwrap();
    }
}
```

This task waits asynchronously for incoming data, then echoes it back. It consumes no CPU while idle and handles data reliably under concurrent execution.

Timer-Based Scheduling and Delays

Embassy uses its own timer abstraction, and it integrates directly with the embedded hardware's SysTick, RTC, or general-purpose timers.

For example, to debounce a button or delay an operation:

```
#[embassy_executor::task]
async fn debounce_button(pin: Input<'static, impl
Pin>) {
    loop {
        pin.wait_for_low().await;

Timer::after(Duration::from_millis(50)).await;

        if pin.is_low() {
            defmt::info!("Button pressed!");
        }
    }
}
```

This kind of logic is simple to express with async, but messy and error-prone with polling or interrupts alone.

Static Memory and No Heap

Embassy does not require dynamic allocation. All memory is statically allocated and checked at compile time.

However, because async state machines must live across `.await` points, you'll need to use `'static` lifetimes for peripheral and task references. This is why peripherals are passed using `'static` and sometimes must be stored in `static mut` with the `#[embassy_executor::task]` macro managing borrowing safely.

This ensures safety and predictability, even under concurrency.

Error Handling in Async Firmware

Since `.await` returns `Result<T, E>` in many drivers, you can handle errors using pattern matching or `?`.

```
let result = uart.write(b"hello").await;


match result {

    Ok(_) => defmt::info!("Sent"),

    Err(e) => defmt::warn!("UART error: {:?}", e),

}
```

In production, you may implement retries, backoff strategies, or hardware resets—all within an async control loop.

When to Use Embassy

Embassy is especially useful when your firmware needs:

Timed tasks or scheduling without blocking

Multiple concurrent operations (e.g., blinking, UART, sensor reading)

Simplified peripheral coordination without ISR complexity

Clean, modular logic for state machines and device protocols

If you're building anything non-trivial—especially with user input, radio protocols, sensors, or power management—Embassy's async structure will save you significant effort.

Async embedded programming with Embassy represents a significant evolution in how we write real-time firmware. By combining Rust's memory safety with cooperative multitasking and peripheral drivers, Embassy lets you build embedded systems that are more readable, reliable, and responsive—without sacrificing performance or predictability.

It replaces complex interrupt juggling with clean tasks and awaitable timers. It brings structured concurrency to `no_std` applications. And it's quickly becoming one of the most forward-looking frameworks in the embedded Rust ecosystem.

Whether you're rewriting a multitask RTOS-based project or starting a new low-power IoT application, Embassy gives you the building blocks to do it right—with fewer bugs and a lot more control.

Supporting OTA (Over-the-Air) Updates

One of the most valuable features you can add to a connected embedded system is the ability to update its firmware without physically accessing the device. Whether your microcontroller is tucked into a sensor box in the middle of a farm, installed inside a smart appliance, or deployed across dozens of industrial machines, the reality is the same: walking around with a USB cable or SWD programmer doesn't scale.

Over-the-Air (OTA) updates give you the power to fix bugs, add features, and improve security post-deployment. Supporting OTA in embedded Rust means combining your firmware with a safe bootloader, managing flash memory carefully, and implementing a robust update protocol.

Core Components of an OTA System

An effective OTA update system typically includes:

A bootloader that selects between firmware images based on metadata (e.g., valid or invalid flag, version number).

Two firmware slots—one active, one standby—to allow safe rollback if the new firmware fails to boot.

An update mechanism that receives firmware (e.g., via UART, BLE, Wi-Fi, LoRa), stores it in flash, and marks it ready.

A verification system that checks integrity before switching to the new firmware (e.g., CRC, SHA256, or signature).

A rollback mechanism in case the new firmware crashes or fails during boot.

Flash Layout for Dual-Firmware Architecture

To support OTA, you need to partition flash memory into distinct regions. A typical flash map might look like this on a 512KB microcontroller:

```
0x0800_0000  ────────────────────────────┐
                Bootloader (32KB)    │
0x0800_8000  ────────────────────────────┘
                App Slot A (224KB)
0x0804_8000  ────────────────────────────
                App Slot B (224KB)
0x0808_8000  ────────────────────────────
                Metadata, State Flags, CRC (32KB)
```

Both App A and App B are fully independent firmware binaries. The bootloader lives in the first sector and is responsible for loading the correct image based on metadata stored in the last page of flash.

You must ensure your linker scripts (`memory.x`) align with this layout so each firmware image is built for the correct offset.

Writing the Bootloader

A minimal Rust-based bootloader might use a configuration like:

```
/* bootloader/memory.x */
```

```
MEMORY

{

   FLASH : ORIGIN = 0x08000000, LENGTH = 32K

   RAM    : ORIGIN = 0x20000000, LENGTH = 40K

}
```

In the bootloader code:

```
#[entry]
fn main() -> ! {
    let state = read_update_state();

    if state.valid_image_b {
        jump_to(0x0804_8000);
    } else {
        jump_to(0x0800_8000);
    }
}
```

The `jump_to()` function performs a raw jump to the reset vector of the target application:

```
unsafe fn jump_to(addr: u32) -> ! {
    let sp = *(addr as *const u32);
    let reset = *((addr + 4) as *const u32);

    let jump: extern "C" fn() -> ! =
core::mem::transmute(reset);


cortex_m::peripheral::SCB::set_vector_table_offset(
addr);
    cortex_m::asm::bootload(sp, jump)
}
```

You must ensure the vector table and stack pointer are reinitialized correctly before executing the target firmware.

Receiving and Writing Updates

Let's assume your device receives firmware over UART, in chunks. The update task might look like this:

```
#[task]
async fn ota_update(mut uart: Uart, flash: &mut
FlashWriter) {
    let mut buffer = [0u8; 256];
    let mut offset = 0;

    loop {
        let len = uart.read(&mut
buffer).await.unwrap();

        flash.write_to_slot_b(offset,
&buffer[..len]).unwrap();
        offset += len;

        if offset >= EXPECTED_IMAGE_SIZE {
            break;
        }
    }

    let checksum =
calculate_crc_from_slot_b(offset);
    mark_firmware_b_valid(checksum);
}
```

This async task receives 256-byte blocks and writes them to App Slot B. After the final block, it calculates the checksum and sets a "ready" flag in the metadata region.

Boot Metadata and Flags

Use a flash-resident struct in a known sector to store update state:

```
#[repr(C)]
pub struct BootState {
    pub app_a_valid: bool,
    pub app_b_valid: bool,
    pub current_app: AppSlot,
    pub new_app: Option<AppSlot>,
    pub crc_b: u32,
}
```

```
#[derive(Copy, Clone)]
pub enum AppSlot {
    A,
    B,
}
```

Store this at a fixed address (e.g., 0x0808_0000) and use CRC protection or signatures to ensure it hasn't been corrupted.

Swapping Firmware After Reboot

When the device resets, the bootloader reads the metadata:

If App B is marked valid, it boots into Slot B.

If not, it falls back to Slot A.

Once App B boots successfully, it should:

Set App B as "confirmed"

Optionally invalidate App A

Reset the metadata to reflect the new boot state

This provides **rollback safety**: if App B crashes or fails to boot, the bootloader returns to App A on the next reboot.

Verifying Firmware Integrity

It's critical to validate the new firmware before running it.

You can use CRC32 or SHA256.

Sign the image if your bootloader includes crypto.

Include a checksum in a header appended to the firmware image.

Example CRC check:

```
fn verify_image(slot: AppSlot, size: usize,
expected_crc: u32) -> bool {
    let start_addr = match slot {
        AppSlot::A => 0x0800_8000,
        AppSlot::B => 0x0804_8000,
```

```
    };

    let data = unsafe {
core::slice::from_raw_parts(start_addr as *const
u8, size) };
    let actual_crc = crc32(data);

    actual_crc == expected_crc
}
```

This lets your bootloader make an informed decision about which image is safe to boot.

Real-World OTA Examples

Let's say you're building an agriculture sensor node with LoRa connectivity. You want to periodically check for a firmware update sent from a central server. You might:

Use a LoRaWAN downlink to trigger an update session.

Start a packet receiver task.

Store packets to flash incrementally.

Verify and apply the update on the next reboot.

Alternatively, on BLE devices, you can use DFU protocols like **Secure DFU** (used by Nordic devices) with your own Rust firmware writing logic.

Precautions and Best Practices

Always reserve a metadata sector for boot state and validate it before use.

Use a watchdog timer during firmware boot to detect crashes.

Avoid writing flash too frequently—respect sector alignment and erase-before-write rules.

Never erase the bootloader in-field unless you're using a dual-boot recovery strategy.

Keep bootloader code as small and robust as possible.

OTA support transforms your embedded firmware from a static, burned-in product to a flexible, remotely upgradeable platform. It adds complexity, yes—but the benefits in maintainability, safety, and user experience are huge.

With Rust's strong type system, you can safely coordinate flash updates, implement strict metadata checks, and avoid the kinds of undefined behaviors that often plague C-based bootloaders. Combined with features like Embassy for async data handling and defmt for structured logs, Rust gives you the tools to build OTA systems that are efficient, robust, and maintainable from first flash to production deployments.

This is the kind of system that lets you scale confidently—whether you're deploying ten units or ten thousand.

RISC-V and Other Architectures in Rust

The embedded systems industry has long been dominated by ARM Cortex-M processors. They're reliable, efficient, and well-supported. But in recent years, **RISC-V** has emerged as a compelling open alternative: free from licensing fees, highly customizable, and increasingly available in silicon from major manufacturers. And thanks to Rust's portability and architecture-agnostic tooling, you're not limited to ARM-based microcontrollers. You can write, build, and flash firmware for **RISC-V** and other architectures—such as ESP32, RP2040, or even x86-based embedded boards—using nearly the same workflow and code structure you've already learned.

RISC-V is a clean-slate instruction set architecture (ISA). Unlike ARM, which is proprietary and requires licensing, RISC-V is **open-source** and maintained by a collaborative consortium. This makes it ideal for academic use, low-cost embedded designs, and custom silicon.

In practice, RISC-V brings several benefits:

No licensing costs for vendors, which can lead to lower device prices.

Custom extensions to tailor chips for AI, DSP, crypto, or ultra-low power.

Open toolchains and documentation, enabling better community support.

Cross-vendor compatibility, not tied to a single company.

From a Rust developer's perspective, the great news is: RISC-V is **well-supported in Rust**, and it's getting better with every release.

Choosing a RISC-V Target

Rust supports multiple RISC-V target triples. The one you'll typically use for embedded microcontrollers is:

```
riscv32imac-unknown-none-elf
```

This stands for:

```
riscv32: 32-bit RISC-V CPU
```

`imac`: Instruction set extensions (Integer, Multiplication/Division, Atomic, Compressed)

`unknown`: Vendor-neutral

`none`: No OS

`elf`: Uses standard ELF binary format

Other possible targets include:

`riscv32i-unknown-none-elf`: For CPUs with only the base integer instruction set.

`riscv64gc-unknown-linux-gnu`: For Linux-capable 64-bit RISC-V SoCs.

To install the embedded target:

```
rustup target add riscv32imac-unknown-none-elf
```

Setting Up a RISC-V Firmware Project

Let's build a basic "blinky" firmware for a RISC-V board such as the **HiFive1 Rev B** or **Longan Nano**.

1. Define Your Cargo Project

```
cargo new --bin riscv-firmware
cd riscv-firmware
```

2. Configure the Target in `.cargo/config.toml`

```toml
[build]

target = "riscv32imac-unknown-none-elf"
```

3. Define the Memory Map in `memory.x`

```
MEMORY
{
    FLASH : ORIGIN = 0x20000000, LENGTH = 512K
    RAM   : ORIGIN = 0x80000000, LENGTH = 64K
}
```

This layout varies depending on the chip. You can typically find the right addresses in your microcontroller's datasheet or the BSP (board support package) crate.

Adding Dependencies

In your `Cargo.toml`, include the RISC-V runtime and HAL:

```toml
[dependencies]

riscv = "0.10"

riscv-rt = "0.11"

embedded-hal = "0.2"

longan-nano = "0.3"  # or another board-specific
crate

panic-halt = "0.2"
```

A Simple Blinky Program on Longan Nano

```rust
#![no_std]
#![no_main]

use longan_nano::hal::{
    pac,
    prelude::*,
    delay::McycleDelay,
```

```
};
use longan_nano::entry;
use panic_halt as _;

#[entry]
fn main() -> ! {
    let dp = pac::Peripherals::take().unwrap();

    let mut rcc = dp.RCC.constrain();
    let clocks = rcc.cfgr.freeze();

    let mut gpio = dp.GPIOA.split(&mut rcc.ahb);
    let mut led = gpio.pa5.into_push_pull_output();

    let mut delay =
McycleDelay::new(clocks.sysclk().0);

    loop {
        led.set_high().unwrap();
        delay.delay_ms(500);
        led.set_low().unwrap();
        delay.delay_ms(500);
    }
}
```

This code:

Initializes the Longan Nano's GPIO and clock configuration.

Blinks an LED on PA5 every 500ms.

Uses the cycle counter for delay.

You can build it using:

```
cargo build --release
```

And flash it using `dfu-util`, `openocd`, or `probe-rs` depending on your setup.

Supported Boards and HALs for RISC-V in Rust

Several RISC-V boards already have working support with HALs and BSPs:

Longan Nano: `longan-nano` crate using the GD32VF103 chip

HiFive1 Rev B: `e310x-hal` crate

Kendryte K210: experimental support with `k210-hal`

ESP32-C3: RISC-V core with Wi-Fi/BLE, supported by `esp-hal` crate

Lichee RV Nano: community-supported via custom linker and HAL setups

Each board typically has:

A PAC crate generated via `svd2rust`

A board crate (like `longan-nano`) wrapping initialization

A HAL implementing `embedded-hal` traits

Use the community-maintained <u>awesome-embedded-rust</u> list to discover current support.

Writing Architecture-Agnostic Code

If you want to write firmware that supports both ARM and RISC-V targets, keep your hardware abstraction separate from your application logic.

For example, define your own trait interface:

```
pub trait Led {

    fn on(&mut self);

    fn off(&mut self);

}
```

Then implement it per-board:

```
#[cfg(target_arch = "arm")]
impl Led for stm32_hal::GpioPin {
    fn on(&mut self) { self.set_high().unwrap(); }
    fn off(&mut self) { self.set_low().unwrap(); }
}

#[cfg(target_arch = "riscv32")]
```

```
impl Led for
longan_nano::hal::gpio::gpiob::PB5<Output<PushPull>
> {
    fn on(&mut self) { self.set_high().unwrap(); }
    fn off(&mut self) { self.set_low().unwrap(); }
}
```

Now your `main()` logic is portable:

```
fn blink_loop<L: Led>(led: &mut L) {
    loop {
        led.on();
        delay_ms(500);
        led.off();
        delay_ms(500);
    }
}
```

This lets you reuse most of your codebase across architectures.

Tooling for RISC-V Debugging

Rust's RISC-V support works with standard tools:

GDB: Use `riscv64-unknown-elf-gdb`

OpenOCD: With a RISC-V interface script

probe-rs: Experimental support for some RISC-V boards

dfu-util: Flash via USB DFU bootloader

For example:

```
openocd -f interface/jlink.cfg -f target/riscv.cfg
```

Then attach with:

```
riscv64-unknown-elf-gdb target/riscv32imac-unknown-
none-elf/release/firmware
(gdb) target remote :3333
```

You can set breakpoints, inspect registers, and single-step as you would on ARM.

Supporting RISC-V in Rust isn't a separate skill—it's a natural extension of what you've already learned. The tools, crate ecosystem, and patterns remain consistent. Once you understand the basic runtime, memory layout, and HAL structure, you can write safe, portable firmware for a whole new class of microcontrollers.

As RISC-V continues to gain traction, having Rust support puts you ahead of the curve. You'll be ready to explore new chips, new use cases, and even contribute upstream to new HALs and community projects. Whether you're working on a new design or porting an existing one, Rust gives you the structure and safety you need across architectures.

Contributing to the Embedded Rust Ecosystem

If you've made it this far into the book, you're no longer just using embedded Rust—you've likely built full applications, integrated with peripherals, debugged hardware quirks, and packaged firmware for real devices. You've also seen how well the ecosystem is maturing, with community-maintained hardware abstraction layers, device crates, bootloaders, logging tools, and testing frameworks.

What makes embedded Rust truly special is that much of this infrastructure is developed, maintained, and improved by people like you—developers who've used the tools in real projects and are motivated to improve them for everyone. Whether you're writing code, fixing typos, testing on a new board, documenting APIs, or publishing reusable drivers, you can have a direct, meaningful impact.

Start with Real Use Cases

One of the most valuable things you can bring to the ecosystem is perspective from real-world usage. Most embedded Rust contributors aren't full-time library maintainers—they're developers who ran into a missing feature, undocumented behavior, or bug while building an actual firmware project. This is often the best starting point.

If you're writing firmware and:

A crate doesn't work on your chip variant

Documentation is unclear or missing

A driver is incomplete or outdated

A build step is too complex

—then you're in the perfect position to help.

Start by opening a **GitHub issue**. Be clear, respectful, and specific. Include your hardware details, versions used, what you expected to happen, and what happened instead. You don't have to propose a fix—just helping identify and describe the problem accurately is already a huge contribution.

Read and Improve Documentation

Rust is well-known for its emphasis on great documentation. But in embedded projects, documentation often lags behind the code—especially in hardware abstraction layers and device-specific crates.

You can contribute by:

Adding code examples for functions or modules

Clarifying confusing or undocumented behavior

Writing a usage guide for a peripheral

Expanding README files with real setup steps

For example, suppose you successfully get I2C running on a new board using the `stm32f4xx-hal` crate. You can contribute that example back to the crate's documentation, so the next developer has something concrete to start from.

You don't need permission. Fork the repository, make your improvement, and submit a **pull request (PR)**. Most maintainers welcome this kind of contribution, and you'll often get friendly feedback quickly.

Contribute Fixes and Features

If you spot a bug in a HAL crate, or you need support for a missing feature (say, PWM output or DMA transfer), consider writing the fix yourself.

Start by cloning the repository and studying its structure. Most HAL crates follow the same conventions:

A device-specific **Peripheral Access Crate (PAC)** generated from an SVD file using `svd2rust`

A HAL layer that wraps the PAC and implements `embedded-hal` traits

Examples and integration tests

For instance, if `stm32f1xx-hal` is missing `set_duty()` for PWM on a particular timer, you can implement that based on the reference manual and submit it upstream.

If you're not sure how to structure the patch, just open an issue first and ask. The maintainers will often guide you toward a clean implementation and help you get it merged.

Publish Your Own Crates

Have you written a custom driver for a sensor like the BME680, a LoRa radio module, or an LED matrix? You can turn that into a reusable crate and publish it to crates.io.

Use the `embedded-hal` traits where possible so others can use it across HALs and boards.

Here's a minimal example of a reusable I2C sensor driver:

```
pub struct MySensor<I2C> {
    i2c: I2C,
    address: u8,
}

impl<I2C, E> MySensor<I2C>
where
    I2C:
embedded_hal::blocking::i2c::WriteRead<Error = E> +
embedded_hal::blocking::i2c::Write<Error = E>,
{
    pub fn new(i2c: I2C, address: u8) -> Self {
        Self { i2c, address }
    }

    pub fn read_data(&mut self) -> Result<u16, E> {
        let mut buf = [0u8; 2];
```

```
        self.i2c.write_read(self.address, &[0x01],
&mut buf)?;
        Ok(u16::from_be_bytes(buf))
    }
}
```

Then, add documentation and publish:

```
cargo login

cargo publish
```

Once it's live, link to it from the awesome-embedded-rust list or share it in the community chat.

Join Community Spaces

You don't need to go it alone. There are active and friendly community spaces where embedded Rust developers collaborate:

Zulip Chat: https://rust-lang.zulipchat.com/#narrow/stream/270262-embedded

Matrix rooms: Look for `#rust-embedded` channels

GitHub Discussions: Many crates have open discussion forums for questions and design planning

Working Group Meetings: The Rust Embedded WG occasionally hosts open meetings where you can listen in or participate

These are great places to:

Ask for help or review

Coordinate a contribution

Find beginner-friendly issues

Share what you've built

Help Maintain or Port Crates

As more chips enter the market—RISC-V, ESP32, newer STM32 variants—the need for board support and HAL ports grows. Many PACs and HALs need active maintainers. If you use a chip that isn't yet fully supported, you can:

Port an existing HAL to a new variant

Generate a PAC from the manufacturer's SVD file

Add support for new peripherals

These efforts often start with one developer creating a working fork, then submitting it as a PR to the parent repo.

Even helping test on your board is useful. If someone adds support for STM32G4 but doesn't have the hardware to verify, you can clone their branch, flash it, and confirm it works. This kind of feedback helps move patches forward.

Track RFCs and Ecosystem Plans

The embedded Rust ecosystem is growing and occasionally evolves in coordinated ways. Keep an eye on:

The embedded Rust RFC repo

Crate changelogs and upcoming major versions (e.g., `embedded-hal` 1.0)

Tooling developments like `probe-rs`, `embassy`, `defmt`, and `cargo-embed`

If you see an RFC for a change (e.g., new I2C traits), read it and comment with your feedback—especially if you've built real-world firmware. The more practical input maintainers receive, the better the ecosystem becomes.

How to Start Today

You don't need a master plan. You can contribute today by doing any of the following:

Improve a README where an example was missing

Open an issue to report something that broke

Fork and patch a HAL to fix one feature you needed

Write a blog post or tutorial explaining how you got something working

Review pull requests if you're familiar with a crate

Ask to co-maintain a driver that seems abandoned

Open-source projects live or die by contributor engagement. Even your first contribution—whether it's a fix, a test, or a question—makes a difference.

Contributing to the embedded Rust ecosystem isn't about having all the answers—it's about sharing what you've learned, improving what you use, and collaborating with others who care about safe, modern firmware development. Whether you're adding support for a new chip, publishing a driver, or just writing better docs, your contribution matters.

The embedded Rust community is practical, welcoming, and always looking for new voices and helpers. As you continue building your projects, remember that the same tools that helped you can be improved by you. This is how we build better embedded systems—not just alone, but together.

www.ingramcontent.com/pod-product-compliance
Lightning Source LLC
La Vergne TN
LVHW081525050326
832903LV00025B/1625